INCLUSALYTICS

HOW DIVERSITY, EQUITY, AND INCLUSION LEADERS USE DATA TO DRIVE THEIR WORK

Victoria Mattingly, PhD
Sertrice Grice, MS
Allison Goldstein

MATTINGLY
SOLUTIONS

This book may be purchased in bulk for business or educational use. Mattingly Solutions is also available for keynote talks aligned with concepts in this book. For more information, contact info@mattinglysolutions.com

To reference this research in academic work, please use the following citation:

Mattingly, V., Grice, S., Goldstein, A. (2022). Inclusalytics: How diversity, equity, and inclusion leaders use data to drive their work. Mattingly Solutions.

FIRST EDITION

Designed by Ian White www.ianpauljameswhite.com

Library of Congress Cataloging-in-Publication Data has been applied for.

ISBN: 979-8-75-013369-7

Imprint: Independently published

ACKNOWLEDGEMENTS

We want to thank everyone who spoke with us for this book. Your stories and expertise are what brought these chapters to life! We would like to thank Kelsie Colley for lending her psychometric expertise to our analysis chapter, Julie Chen and Sarah Jackson for helping with citations and graphics throughout the book, and Camaria Lehman for keeping the day-to-day business of Mattingly Solutions on track as we were elbows-deep in writing and revisions. Thanks to our launch team and early readers who took time to help us get the word out about Inclusalytics. Thanks also to our family and friends for their support and encouragement as we undertook this daunting project.

Lastly, a special thanks to *you,* our readers. Thank you for taking the time to learn about and (hopefully) committing to take a more data-driven approach to creating more diverse, equitable, and inclusive workplaces. Your efforts to make this work measurable and replicable are what will ultimately help us build workplaces—and a world—where *everyone* has the opportunity to thrive.

TABLE OF CONTENTS

PART III: DATA-DRIVEN INTERVENTIONS: TURN INSIGHTS INTO ACTIONS

PREFACE

By Victoria Mattingly, PhD (Dr. V) and Sertrice Grice, MS

This was not supposed to be our first book. Our first book was going to be about allyship—a book not just for diversity, equity, and inclusion (DEI) leaders, but for *anyone* wanting to be a better human at work. Between the two of us, we have written a PhD dissertation on allyship and have given numerous keynotes, trainings, and webinars on the topic. However, when the DEI space blew up in 2020, we quickly realized that the world was not quite ready for allyship. Most organizations and leaders needed more foundational and strategic DEI support first.

With so many organizations just getting started on their DEI journeys, we found ourselves going back to the basics. Companies were not coming to us asking how they could better engage overrepresented group members to leverage their power and status for good (i.e., allyship). Instead, they were asking:

"How do we know if we're 'moving the needle' when it comes to DEI?"

"How will we know if our DEI programs and interventions actually have impact?"

"How can we assess the ROI of our DEI efforts?"

We wrote this book as a way to answer those questions. Importantly, we wrote this book as a way that *you*, our reader, can answer those questions using *your organization's data*. "Data," as you'll come to find, is the operative word. Like everything we do when it comes to DEI, we started with research. We interviewed dozens of DEI leaders to find out how they use data to build more diverse, equitable, and inclusive organizations.

Our interviewees worked at startups, midsize organizations, and global companies with tens of thousands of employees. They spanned numerous industries, from retail to construction, academia to healthcare, tech to nonprofit. Some of these leaders were just beginning their DEI journey. Others were new to a formalized DEI role. And still others had been doing this work in their organization for quite some time. In sum, we made a point to interview a representative sample of those doing DEI "on the ground" so we could speak to a variety of contexts and examples of building more diverse, equitable, and inclusive organizations.

We also pulled from our academic roots. As industrial-organizational (I-O) psychologists who are passionate about and trained in improving the human experience in the workplace, we didn't just want to tell you what we're doing with our clients (although we provide plenty of examples); we wanted to share the research behind those—and many other—practices of gathering and analyzing DEI data and putting those insights to work. So that's what we did.

Although I-O psychology is the foundation of our work, we did not want this book to be written *by* I-O psychologists *for* I-O psychologists. Rather, we wanted this book to be a tool for DEI, HR, and organizational leaders seeking to take a more data-driven approach to their DEI work. That's why we brought in our third author, Allison Goldstein. Allison has written numerous books, articles, reports, and white papers, and has edited many more. She took our I-O jargon and technical approach to DEI and helped to create a book that is more practical, relatable, and dare we say *enjoyable* to read. We are eternally grateful to her for taking our words, ideas, and expertise and turning them into something we are proud to share with the world.

Now, who will benefit most from *Inclusalytics*? First and foremost, this book is for those of you building and leading diversity, equity, and inclusion efforts at your organization. This includes, but is not limited to:

- DEI practitioners looking for best practices and guidance on how to get started
- HR practitioners who are overseeing DEI or assisting their DEI colleagues
- Senior leaders who are supporting DEI leaders and want to understand the process
- People-analytics professionals seeking a resource to help educate the DEI practitioners with whom they are partnering
- DEI consultants who want to better support their clients
- Anyone else curious about how to take a more data-driven approach to DEI

We want to point out that although the data collection, analysis strategies, and the interventions we recommend can be useful to organizations operating within any culture, this book does take a mostly US-centric lens to DEI. Most of our clients are US-based, as are the DEI leaders we interviewed for the book. Future editions will include more multicultural examples and perspectives.

Inclusalytics is the process of applying statistics to DEI data to detect patterns, make predictions, select evidence-based interventions, and assess the impact of those interventions to advance workplace inclusion. In short, it's using data to measure and drive inclusive behaviors.

By reading this book, you will start seeing diversity, equity, and inclusion less as "warm and fuzzy" ideals. "Making everyone feel welcome" so people can "bring their most authentic selves to work" will increasingly sound more like platitudes, and you'll start seeing that "moving the needle" requires real, tangible metrics. That's because we're going to teach you to see DEI as hard numbers that need to be gathered, closely monitored, and used as empirical evidence to demonstrate the impact—or lack thereof—of your DEI efforts on *all* people in your organization.

The book begins with a brief overview of diversity, equity, and inclusion to get us all on the same page. We then help you identify what data to collect, how to collect it, and a few high-level techniques you can use to analyze it. From there we share how to turn your analysis into insights and those insights into data-driven interventions. Finally, we close the book by looking to the future of using data to foster DEI within organizations . . . i.e., Inclusalytics! We've also included a glossary of all important terms that are **bolded** the first time they appear in each chapter. And if all that wasn't enough, we also built you an Inclusalytics Workbook[1] you can immediately use to apply lessons from the book directly to your work as a DEI leader.

Our vision for the DEI consulting firm[2] we co-lead is to improve the human experience at work for one billion employees worldwide. This book takes a step toward that goal by offering a sustainable, evidence-based approach to increasing DEI inside organizations. There's a saying that what gets measured, gets done. DEI is no different. May this book provide you the direction and inspiration to start down the data-driven path to a more diverse, equitable, and inclusive workplace.

---

1   Get your free copy of our Inclusalytics Workbook at www.inclusalytics.com/workbook

2   Learn more about our DEI work at www.mattinglysolutions.com

PART I:

THE WHY AND WHAT
(AND A LITTLE HOW)
OF INCLUSALYTICS

CHAPTER 1:
Why DEI and Measurement Matter

If you're reading this book, we don't need to sell you on the merits of **diversity**, **equity**, and **inclusion** (which we'll refer to from now on by the well-known acronym **DEI**)—you obviously have a stake in it. You know that more racially diverse, ethnically diverse, and gender-diverse companies outperform their competitors. You've seen that employees who feel a sense of **belonging** enjoy their work more, perform better, and stick around longer. In short, you know DEI matters, and you're invested in helping advance it in your organization.

What we might need to convince you (or your executive leaders) of, however, is why you should *measure* DEI—specifically why it matters to measure DEI in the same, rigorous, impartial way you measure other critical business objectives. You'd never look around the office, see smiling faces, and think, "Well, I guess our profitability is fine." You also wouldn't assume that because you haven't personally heard any complaints, customer loyalty and satisfaction are as strong as ever. DEI is no different from business measures like revenue or net promoter score. And if you understand the business case (not to mention the *moral* case) for investing in DEI—and again, since you elected to pick up this book, we assume you do—then the only logical conclusion is that DEI should also be tracked, measured, evaluated, and continually improved in the same systematic way as other business metrics and goals. After all, revenue growth goals only make sense in relationship to year-over-year growth. Customer loyalty is meant to be strengthened and satisfaction improved. There are no endpoints for these measures, and there are no endpoints for DEI either!

Ultimately our proposition is this: First, it's important to collect, analyze, and derive actionable insights from DEI data so you know how to best direct your DEI efforts. Then, it's just as important to continue collecting and analyzing data in order to measure your ongoing progress toward DEI objectives. This is how you ensure that the work you are doing is having an impact ... and course correct when it's not.

In short, data is the answer to advancing DEI—if you know what to do with it.

The term "**Inclusalytics**," which you may have been wondering about (given that it's the title of this book), has to do with the intersection of DEI and data. Specifically, Inclusalytics is the process of applying statistics to DEI data to detect patterns, make predictions, select evidence-based interventions, and assess the impact of those interventions to advance workplace inclusion. We use *a lot* of Inclusalytics methods in our work, many of which we'll introduce throughout the book.

So now that we've piqued your interest, a quick disclaimer: this book is not going to give you quick and easy answers. It's not going to tell you exactly what metrics "every company needs to track" or "how to improve DEI at your business in thirty days." Prescriptive advice like that requires delving into the specific dynamics in which you, your executives, and your workforce are operating. Anyone who claims they can deliver DEI results without partnering with you to do that work is selling something they can't deliver.

What we *are* going to do is guide you through the process of figuring out how to use facts, figures, surveys, interviews, **focus groups**, human resource information system (HRIS) data, and more to quantify—and improve—DEI at your organization. Our aim in this book is to help you answer questions like:

"What diversity data should I be looking at?"

"How do I measure equity?"

"How can I use survey data to measure workplace inclusion?"

Of course, the answers to these questions will vary based on your organization's specific constraints and needs. Therefore, we're not only going to help get you started but also show you what other businesses and organizations are doing. Based on the many interviews we've conducted, we will share how leaders measure, monitor, and adjust their DEI strategies in ways that allow them to pivot and iterate their approach—not based on the latest trends, but according to *their* company's data.[1] Because, as DEI science progresses, evidence-based best practices will inevitably change over time. It's important to develop robust, data-backed strategies that can adapt to shifts in your organization's workforce and unique DEI needs.

---

1   Practice your talking points about how measuring DEI can benefit *your* organization in Worksheet #1 of our Inclusalytics Workbook, available at www.inclusalytics.com/workbook

Of course, this book is called *Inclusalytics*, not DEI-alytics. So we want to say up front: yes, inclusion is our main focus. Diversity and equity still matter—they matter a lot—but diversity without inclusion is window dressing, and equity can't be achieved until all identities are considered and included. Inclusion is the link tying DEI together. It's what will ultimately enable companies to make lasting, impactful changes that move them toward becoming a more diverse and equitable organization. That is why inclusion—specifically the intersection of inclusion and data—is the main focus of our book.

That being said, we're still going to talk about diversity—it's a big part of what companies can measure to see whether their inclusion efforts are on track or not—and we're going to touch on equity, too. To accomplish all of that, we need to be on the same page in our understanding of what these terms mean. Moreover, **operationalizing** terms—clearly defining them specific to how they will be discussed and measured—is a crucial first step in any culture change initiative or behavioral change intervention. So, while the next chapter may seem a bit remedial if you do DEI work day in and day out, bear with us. Because getting on the same page when it comes to what we mean by "diversity," "equity," and "inclusion" is a crucial—and often overlooked—first step in any DEI initiative.

CHAPTER 2:
Defining DEI

You've probably heard the terms "**diversity**," "**equity**," and "**inclusion**" thrown around for so long, you feel like you have a clear understanding of what these words mean. What we've seen in our work, however, is that it's easy for even **DEI** experts to conflate these terms and treat them interchangeably—and they are *not* synonymous.

Two of us authors are **industrial-organizational** (I-O) psychologists, meaning we were trained to use science to improve the human experience at work.[2] In our world of I-O psychology, we call the lack of clarity around DEI terminology **construct confusion**. Essentially, if we can't agree upon these words' distinctive meanings, then we don't have a shared language to even begin to address the issues that are preventing organizations from building more diverse, inclusive, and equitable cultures and workspaces. So, since this book is all about using data to uncover DEI issues and achieve tangible year-after-year results, let's begin by laying down some definitions.

Diversity: How We See Each Other

Diversity is the presence (and amount) of difference within a group in a given setting. For our purposes, that setting is work, so the more different races, ethnicities, genders, cultural backgrounds, etc. that are present in a workplace, the more diverse that workplace is.

A few important points about the term "diverse":

(1) An individual cannot be diverse, because diversity only exists at the *group* level. Therefore, saying someone is a "diverse candidate" or a "diverse hire" is inadvisable, as this could quickly devolve into **tokenism** (more on that shortly). When referring to an individual who is not part of the overrepresented group,

---

2   To learn more about I-O psychology, check out www.SIOP.org

use terms like "underrepresented" or "historically disadvantaged" rather than "diverse" or "minority." The latter terms infer a "less-than" place in societal and organizational hierarchies. Furthermore, having a diverse organization goes beyond finding just one person from a particular identity, but having a meaningful distribution of identities (i.e., one person out of a thousand isn't diversity).

(2) Diversity is *not* a code word for one specific demographic—which we'll also call "identity"—of people (e.g., Black, Indigenous, People of Color [**BIPOC**], LGBTQ+, women), despite how it's been used in recent rhetoric. Take, for example, the societal outcry after the murder of George Floyd in 2020. Many organizations quickly announced they were investing in DEI, but in actuality, all of their efforts focused on anti-Black racism and, specifically, supporting the Black community in the workforce. Companies would then profess, "We are working to diversify our leadership team," when what they really meant was, "We are working to ensure there are more Black people on our leadership team."

To be clear, race is so much more than Black and white, and diversity is so much more than race. Had companies made statements that they were specifically focusing on anti-Black racism, instead of claiming to prioritize DEI, there wouldn't be an issue. But conflating the two leads to confusion and minimizes the impact of each. Defining diversity in a broader (i.e., a more inclusive!) sense is crucial to taking a holistic approach to DEI. That being said, while we will discuss race at times throughout the book, this is not a book on anti-Black racism.[3] We will use examples from various identities and cover a broad view of diversity.

Additionally, even if an organization were to focus on race, doing so at the exclusion of all other identities will lead to incomplete outcomes at best, and false conclusions at worst. No singular identity marker (e.g., race, gender, sexual orientation) exists in isolation from other identity markers. One isn't just a man, but a white, cis, able-bodied individual. Similarly, someone who is gay is not a monolith for all gay people, because sexual orientation is not in isolation from gender, race, education level, caregiving status, and so on. People aren't just one aspect of their identity. Therefore, as convenient as it may be for crunching numbers and writing reports, we must measure multiple defining attributes and their intersections. This is called **intersectionality**.

According to the Oxford Dictionary, intersectionality is "the interconnected nature of social categorizations such as race, class, and gender, regarded as creating overlapping and interdependent systems of **discrimination** or disadvantage." In other words, **privilege** (or lack thereof) and discrimination are conferred by

---

3 Our recommendation for a great book on anti-Black racism is "How to Be An Antiracist" by Ibram X. Kendi.

a whole slew of multiple identities, and those identities cannot be considered independently of one another. The term "intersectionality" was coined in 1989 by American lawyer and civil rights activist Kimberlé Crenshaw as a way to help explain the multifaceted oppression of Black women. While the term has since expanded to include more than just gender and race, Crenshaw's main point was that women are marginalized and Black people are marginalized, and individuals possessing *both* attributes are often subjected to **bias** and violence that go beyond the sum of those two identities. In an interview given to *Time* magazine in 2020, Crenshaw described the term "intersectionality" as,

> *basically a lens, a prism, for seeing the way in which various forms of inequality often operate together and exacerbate each other. We tend to talk about race inequality as separate from inequality based on gender, class, sexuality, or immigrant status. What's often missing is how some people are subject to all of these, and the experience is not just the sum of its parts.*

We will talk more about how to deal with intersectionality from a data perspective in Chapter 8, but the important thing to note is that when you evaluate the diversity of your workforce, looking at identity markers in *combination* with one another is crucial for choosing appropriate interventions that will foster inclusion and equity . . . leading to more overall diversity in the long run.

(3) Notice how we ended the last paragraph with "more overall diversity" rather than "more of one group at the sake of another"? That's because pursuing diversity is not a zero-sum game. Workplace diversity is all about **representation**, or ensuring that your workforce demographics represent the people in your market, your industry, and the population in geographic areas your organization operates. Sometimes when US workers hear the word "diversity" they think anything *but* male and/or white (causing those who identify as white males to commonly feel excluded from DEI efforts). But when thinking in terms of representation (rather than "us versus them"), white men are *absolutely* part of a diverse workforce. Considering that as of 2020, white men make up 43 percent of the working US population, you would expect your workforce to have a similar percentage. When it comes to thinking of diversity in terms of representation, we should *all* see where we fit in that picture.

(4) The final point to make regarding diversity is that in the context of DEI, diversity affects our perceptions of others. Diversity is how we see each other. Okay, you might not be able to "see" that someone is bisexual or a veteran, but once you know how a person identifies on these and other attributes (like gender, race, religion, caregiver status, education, . . . even personality), this is how you see them: as a heterosexual Asian Catholic mother, or a bisexual gender-fluid Gen Z-er. As you will come to discover later in this book, diversity is the easiest to measure and also relatively easy to improve in an organization compared to equity and inclusion. But remember: diversity is what we see. If all you are doing is changing the makeup of your workforce without also changing culture and systems, those changes are unlikely to stick, and you may even end up creating more problems than you started with.

That's why we call it *"diversity, equity, and inclusion,"* after all.

Equity: Elevating Those Who Have Been Historically Left Behind

The next letter in DEI is a tricky one. In fact, if there's one term that we've found people are *least* able to define, it's equity.

We define equity as the intentional rebalancing of power dynamics to result in the fair treatment of *all* employees regarding the accessibility of information, opportunities, and resources. Pursuing equity means detecting and eliminating barriers in an organization's policies, practices, and procedures that prevent individuals (especially those from underrepresented groups) from reaching their potential. However, that's a pretty academic definition, so here's a simple business example to help illustrate what inequity (and an attempt to fix it) actually looks like:

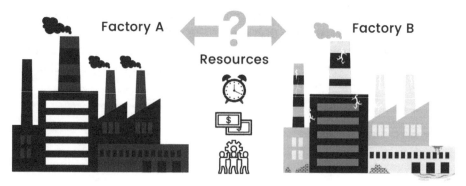

Figure 1

Let's say a manufacturing company has two factories: (See Figure 1) Factory A and Factory B. Factory A is operating at 90 percent effectiveness, and Factory B is operating at 50 percent effectiveness. You have $100,000 in resources that you can apply however you see fit in order to improve your company's margins specific to manufacturing output. If you want to improve your company's overall productivity, it would be foolish to split these resources 50/50 between Factories A and B. The wise thing to do is to put the lion's share of resources into Factory B, where they are needed the most and where you can make more sizable gains.

If we try to reinterpret this example through a DEI-based lens—say, gender—the factories are not men and women; the factories are the systemic barriers that affect the overall success (or lack thereof) of male and female employees, respectively. The factories represent the way the workplace was built to favor men, which inhibits women from reaching their full potential. In other words, the men in Factory A are performing at a better rate than the women in Factory B not because they are men, but because the overall structure in which they are operating systematically favors men over women. The resulting imbalance is why the women in Factory B need—and deserve!—more resources: They are operating at a disadvantage. They are trying to succeed in a system that was not built for their unique situation such as their expected role in society to be the primary caregiver. Research has confirmed that the additional unpaid labor women do compared to men holds them back from advancing in the workplace—a disparity that has only been exacerbated by the COVID-19 pandemic. Systemic issues like these that benefit one group over another are what must be identified and then changed via updated polices, practices, procedures, and overall culture change in order to improve equity in an organization.

An important thing to note regarding equity, however, is that equity is *not* parity—i.e., when all things between groups are equal. When you look at statistics of who is doing what within an organization (say, white people and BIPOC people, or, in our example, Factories A and B), those numbers don't need to be identical. When companies pursue parity in lieu of true equity, they are usually only treating the surface level, or the diversity element of the DEI equation. Equity goes deeper: it's about recognizing that systemic advantages and barriers exist in society, and each person's unique background affects what advantages they enjoy and what barriers they face. Equity isn't as much about an individual's identity as it is about the systems that hinder historically disadvantaged groups from achieving fair outcomes.

To take a more concrete look at the difference between equity and parity, let's turn to an example of everyone's favorite equity issue: compensation. If a man and a woman[4] are working in the same role, yet the man has more job-relevant knowledge, skills, and abilities (KSAs) than the woman, the man will probably earn a higher salary. Given that difference in KSAs, their pay difference would be considered "fair."

An organization pursuing pure parity might see these two employees and decide, "We'd better pay the woman equally so no one thinks we pay men more than women!" Is this equitable? The man is unlikely to think so. And if there's another woman with extensive KSAs earning that same higher salary, and she sees the less experienced woman getting bumped up to her pay grade, she probably won't think it's equitable either.

However, if the man were being paid more than the woman with equal KSAs, this would be an instance of pay inequity. The "advantage" here is not KSAs, but being male. An organization looking to improve gender pay equity should be able to look at the salaries of its employees, their KSAs, their gender, and any other job-relevant criteria, and answer the question, "Are we valuing men and women with the same level of expertise equally?" If not—and there is definitive research showing that, on average, women in the US make $0.82 for every $1 men make, with Black, Native American, and Latina women making even less (remember intersectionality?)—it might be time to give those underpaid women a salary bump (and women of color an even bigger bump!) to match men of similar qualifications.

Inclusion: How We Treat Each Other

The final element of DEI, inclusion, goes beneath the surface of who we are or the structures in which we exist, and is all about what we *do*. Inclusion, in a word, comes down to behaviors.

As we discussed in Chapter 1, we have chosen to focus this book on inclusion because we see it as the glue that holds DEI together. Inclusion is what will enable your DEI efforts to succeed.[5] It is what will change the culture at your organization to ensure that *everyone* has a voice and the opportunity to succeed. It is what will attract more individuals from underrepresented backgrounds to work at your organization and increase the retention of your people, especially those

---

4   We recognize that gender is not a binary construct, but for the purpose of this example we made it binary for simplicity.

5   Break down how DEI is defined at *your* organization in Worksheet #2 of our Inclusalytics Workbook, available at www.inclusalytics.com/workbook

from underrepresented groups. In short, inclusion is a proactive, strategic way to make your workforce more effective, efficient, and productive—all because it is action-oriented.

If it sounds like we're belaboring the importance of inclusion, it's because we really want to hammer home that without inclusion, none of DEI works. Historically, organizations have focused on diversity and turned DEI work into a numbers game: "How many X people work at our company?" "What percentage of the institution is made up of people who are Y?" But getting a certain type of person in the door or onto a team is not enough. Rebecca Baumgartner, senior diversity and inclusion manager at a global labor and employment law firm, described the difference:

> *At my firm, I think the inclusion piece is about being seen and heard as a person and as an attorney who has value to add instead of just as this token ornament that you add as a cherry on top to seal the deal.*

In short, diversity without inclusion can quickly become tokenism, "the practice of doing something (such as hiring a person because they belong to a historically disadvantaged group) only to prevent criticism and give the appearance that people are being treated fairly." What results is "tokenized" people feel undervalued because they're unsure whether they were chosen to fill some sort of quota or for their actual skills and expertise, and they experience other stressors like exacerbated pressure to perform, pressure to assimilate, and social isolation. Meanwhile, everyone else can wind up resentful of the seemingly unwarranted preferential treatment given to colleagues from underrepresented groups.

Clearly, tokenism is a recipe for disaster. First, feeling tokened often causes people not to perform at their best—which affects the organization's bottom line. One reason for this is something called **stereotype threat**: when someone unknowingly confirms a negative stereotype about the marginalized group to which they belong. (Think "women are bad at math" or "Black men are aggressive.") Paradoxically, it's the feelings of fear and anxiety of confirming a stereotype—not their actual talent, intelligence, or ability—that can hurt the quality and efficiency of their work, thereby confirming the stereotype. The other negative consequence of tokenism is that tokens will ultimately leave in search of somewhere that *does* make them feel appreciated for the real value they bring to their work. Losing employees also hurts the organization's bottom line, which we'll expand upon in just a minute.

On the flip side, if you have an inclusive organization, you will naturally attract a more diverse workforce. (Who wouldn't want to work somewhere?) And as you foster inclusive behaviors and make policies more inclusive of everyone, those structures will also be more *equitable*. See? Inclusion truly is the linchpin of DEI.

Inclusive Behaviors

Now, if inclusion is all about behaviors, then what exactly are **inclusive behaviors**? (See Figure 2)

Research-backed inclusive behaviors include encouraging others to bring their authentic selves to work, sincerely inquiring about and learning from others' unique perspectives, and amplifying the thoughts and ideas of marginalized group members. We define inclusive behaviors as the actions that make others feel valued, respected, seen, and heard. When explaining inclusive behaviors to our clients and workshop participants, we often use this three-tier model.

Figure 2

The easiest to implement are behaviors that we refer to as "everyday inclusion." (See Figure 3) For example, **microaffirmations** are small, otherwise innocuous actions that we can take to make others feel valued, respected, seen, and heard. Examples include showing someone that you are actively listening as they speak, turning your body toward someone entering a room, or even a simple smile.

Of course, inclusive behaviors aren't limited to small daily actions; they can go all the way up to big, high-impact actions such as inclusive leadership, **mentorship**, **sponsorship**, and, at the top, allyship. These are terms that, like diversity, equity, and inclusion, can also often get muddled, so if you're unsure of what they mean or how they differ, never fear; we'll define and describe them later in Chapter 13, where we discuss DEI interventions.

Inclusive Behaviors

Everyday Inclusion	Inclusive Leadership	Allyship
Psychological safety	Learning and meeting individual needs	Bystander intervention
Microaffirmations	Holding others accountable for DEI	Sponsorship
Emotional intelligence	Building diverse teams	Activism

Figure 3

This list is, of course, in no way exhaustive. Inclusive behaviors can run the gamut and even include things you *don't* do. Take something like pronouncing an unfamiliar name. If you check with the person and ask how they pronounce it, even if you have to do this a few times (because let's admit it, we've all had to do this), you are being inclusive. You are recognizing that person as a unique individual, and you are demonstrating that you want them to belong to the group in the same way as everyone else whose name you can easily pronounce. On the other hand, if you don't bother to learn the pronunciation of their name, and you consistently mispronounce it or use some other term or nickname you've chosen, then you are performing the inverse of a microaffirmation: a microaggression.

Microaggressions are instances of subtle and indirect discrimination, which can be intentional or unintentional, against marginalized populations. A name might seem like such a small thing, but it represents complex elements of a person's identity, like ethnicity, cultural background, and lineage. By mispronouncing or superseding someone's name, you are devaluing all of those elements of their personhood. And while the "micro" part of microaggression may make it seem small and inconsequential, it is still a form of aggression that harms the person on the receiving end. In fact, the particularly insidious thing about microaggressions is the fact that people perceive them as so inconsequential as to not exist or matter. But they do. And the more microaggressions a person has to deal with over time, the more damage that is done—which is why inclusive behaviors are so important.

For now, what you need to know is that inclusive behaviors are judged as such based on how they make people *feel*. The goal is to make people feel included, but that can mean a lot of different things. Terry Roberts, the chief inclusion and diversity officer at American Eagle Outfitters (AEO), described inclusive behaviors as giving people the feelings of empowerment, freedom, and ownership:

> *When you feel that you are included in something, you feel empowered. I think freedom is another component. When you are included, you have the freedom to be authentic. Lastly, I think you gain a sense of ownership of whatever you're a part of.*

Adam Murray, the US director of diversity, equity, and inclusion at National Grid, echoed the idea of empowerment and added safety to the list:

> *It doesn't have to be an agreeable atmosphere, but one where everyone feels empowered to say what they feel and say and think without fear.*

And the common thread throughout these two definitions, as well as the one provided by Lindsay Ciancetta, PhD, a DEI practitioner, is authenticity:

> *Am I able to be myself, to bring my best self to the table? It's all about that human experience.*

Our favorite definition of inclusion comes from a 2011 paper by Lynn Shore and colleagues—not because it's published in an academic journal (although we're suckers for a good peer-reviewed research article), but because it uses the term that we have found is most apt when understanding inclusion: **belonging**. (See Figure 4) The authors describe inclusion as "the degree to which individuals experience treatment from the group that *satisfies their need for belongingness and uniqueness*" (emphasis added). This definition demonstrates that inclusion and belonging do not exist in a vacuum; employees in a workplace include or exclude others, which impacts the perceptions of those who are the target of that treatment.

Belonging—or the feeling that one's authentic self is valued, respected, seen, and heard—is very much the crux of inclusion and is consequently being added to DEI ("DEIB") more and more in recent years. Unsurprisingly, the idea of belonging came up frequently in our discussions with DEI leaders. Yet through those discussions and through research we've conducted, we have found that belonging often gets lumped in with inclusion so that the terms are used interchangeably. This is a mistake. Inclusion refers to behaviors, while belonging is a feeling that is an *outcome* of inclusive behaviors.

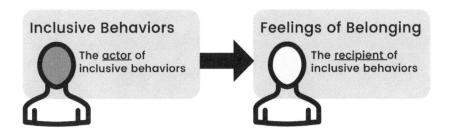

Figure 4

We will dive deeper into how to measure feelings of belonging in Chapters 6 and 7. In the meantime, we're going to present it as part of the model we use when explaining and promoting the value of DEI work—a model that's going to help you build the business case you need to get your DEI efforts off the ground.

CHAPTER 3:

Gaining Executive-Level Buy-In

So far we've covered the *why* and the *what* of **DEI**. Why DEI is important—and why it's important to *measure*—is the bedrock on which this whole book is built. If you've read this far, we assume you've bought into the why (if you weren't already bought in, that is!). Plus, now that you've made it through Chapters 1 and 2, you share our understanding of what DEI is, particularly how **diversity**, **equity**, and **inclusion** differ from yet depend upon each other, and how essential inclusion is to the full DEI picture.

Now we're coming up on the *how*—how to use data to plan, execute, and evaluate DEI initiatives within your organization. Before you can get started pulling HR data and distributing surveys, however, you need something important: senior leader buy-in.

The DEI Equation

We talk to executive leaders nearly every day about the value of DEI work. After all, that's our business! If they don't see the value—the true business value—in what we do, then they won't hire us, and we'll be out of jobs. More importantly, though, they won't give the energy and resources necessary to properly implement and sustain DEI within their organization. Therefore, we've thought a lot about how to make the case for DEI, especially in terms of hard numbers.

Many folks working in DEI will make the case for DEI's moral value. Ensuring that everyone within an organization is treated equitably and feels that they belong is, indeed, the right and ethical thing to do. This argument will appeal to business leaders who are morally driven, although in reality you won't need to "argue" much at all, because these leaders are already bought in.

There is a strong business case, too, though, as research has consistently shown that "diversity pays." In other words, more diverse workforces yield better business results. The relationship between DEI and profitability is essential to demonstrate the return on investment (ROI) of DEI efforts. We're going to spend most of this chapter delving into the business case for DEI, because it's often what is needed to convince senior leaders, even those who see DEI work as a moral imperative, to *systematically measure* DEI the way they do their other key performance indicators (KPIs). (After all, that's what this book is all about!) However, we must first caution against focusing *exclusively* on the business case for DEI. Looking at DEI as "pull X diversity/inclusion/equity levers and Y profits will come out the other side" will come across as cold, compliance-driven, and **performative**, all of which will undermine an organization's DEI efforts. It's important to remember that businesses are made up of *people*, and people are more than numbers.

When making the case for DEI to business leaders, it's best to start simple and big picture and then narrow down to the nitty-gritty facts and figures. After all, if you're following an old-fashioned, pre-Google Maps roadmap, you don't want to look at street names before you generally understand if you'll be traveling north, south, east, or west. We'd therefore like to begin with a very basic equation for understanding DEI.

In Chapter 2, we said that when an organization makes progress toward becoming more diverse, equitable, and inclusive, it gives its workforce—especially those in underrepresented groups—the invaluable sense of **belonging**. That logic yields this equation:

Diversity   Equity   Inclusion

Belonging

Figure 5

What's important to note here is that all three elements on the left side of the equal sign are essential to achieve the outcome on the right. As an example, let's imagine a Latina woman is working at a company. Her colleagues all treat her very inclusively, viewing her as a unique individual and ensuring that her voice is heard in meetings. Because the company values equity, as evidenced by thoughtful policies, practices, and procedures, she is given equal opportunities for advancement and promotion within the organization, such as the flexibility to work from home when her responsibilities as a mother require it. However, she is the only Latina in her business unit, and nearly all of her colleagues are white men. In this situation, the company and its employees have seemingly made every effort to be inclusive, yet this woman will probably not feel that she belongs, because, just by looking around, she sees no one else like herself. The diversity piece is lacking. *All three elements* are crucial for belonging. (See Figure 6)

Now, the question is why should companies care about belonging? After all, feelings are feelings; they're not what make you money. But actually, they do. People who feel like they belong in an organization show higher levels of **engagement** at work (see Figure 5). While academics define engagement as "a positive, fulfilling, work-related state of mind that is characterized by vigor, dedication, and absorption," Gallup defines employee engagement as being "involved in, enthusiastic about and committed to their work and workplace." And why is this metric a central part of what Gallup tracks for so many of its Fortune 500 clientele? Because engagement leads to productivity—and productivity has a serious impact on an organization's bottom line.

As Roberts of AEO put it, when you feel a sense of belonging at work,

> . . . *all of a sudden your experience is going to naturally get more meaningful and you will most likely start to have a better experience. And it is a win from a company's standpoint. You're going to actually like coming to work, you're going to bring more value, and you're going to do a better job.*

In other words, people who feel they belong will not only feel better about what they're doing, where they're doing it, and whom they're doing it with, but they're also going to be more innovative and produce higher-quality work (measured in terms of better products/services and happier customers). And that higher-quality work, or *productivity*, is what C-suite executives are looking for. That's what makes the company money.

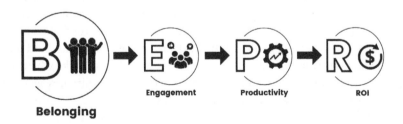

Figure 6

Belonging, engagement, innovation, and productivity (not to mention attracting diverse top talent and keeping those star performers around) are the benefits of DEI work, and they're going to help you make your business case for DEI to senior leadership. Yes, your *business case*. Because no matter how good people's intentions are, no matter how much they want to change the world for the better, at the end of the day, executives are responsible for making money and ensuring that the organizations in their care remain viable.

The connection between DEI and profitability continues to be proven year after year. What you're going to show executives is that DEI can take an organization past viability—it can help it thrive by earning very real, very tangible ROI. (See Figure 6)

Getting Senior Leaders on Board

As we've said, an organization can profess its intentions to become the most diverse, inclusive, and equitable workplace ever, but if the top brass haven't truly bought in—if they're just doing it for appearance's sake or to get shareholders off their backs—then even the best, most well-thought-out DEI strategy is destined to fail. And frankly, there probably won't be a well-thought-out DEI function at all if the C-suite hasn't gotten on board, because there simply won't be resources (money, time, people) to make it happen.

So how do you build your business case for DEI?

Why, with data of course.

The Cost of Turnover

Let's begin with what will happen if your organization doesn't invest in DEI work: people will leave. And when people leave, the organization loses money.

There are two categories of cost related to turnover: losses that are hard to quantify and those that are easy. One hard-to-quantify loss is productivity. When someone leaves an organization, their work must still get done, so it's temporarily distributed among other workers until that role can be refilled. This can overextend employees, which will eventually decrease the overall pace and quality of work being performed. (Think of how easy it is to make a mistake when you're trying to multitask!) On top of that, when someone new is hired, research has shown that it takes them an average of *eight months* to reach an equivalent level of productivity as the employee they're replacing. That's over half a year of lost productivity from just one employee leaving.

Then there's the nebulous cost of losing institutional knowledge. This is difficult to generalize across positions and industries, so here's an example: In the early 2000s, a corroded pipeline in Alaska leaked hundreds of thousands of gallons of oil into the ocean over five days. The environmental destruction notwithstanding, that oil company lost considerable money while it was forced to shut down the pipeline for repairs. Its stock slumped, and it was ultimately fined millions of dollars for its failure to comply with government environmental regulations. There are likely many reasons this leak occurred, but let's suppose that an employee with specialized knowledge of that particular pipeline left the company and had not been replaced. As a result, no one else knew the deterioration that was happening, and so the leak occurred. This thought experiment shows that loss of one person and their institutionalized knowledge can conceivably cost an organization millions, if not billions, of dollars.

There's another even less readily apparent cost to turnover, and that's the impact it has on your brand image. Admittedly, in most situations, one employee leaving an organization won't lead to an environmental catastrophe that creates a PR nightmare of this magnitude. However, if your organization is seeing a lot of turnover, it's not great for the brand at-large. Socially conscious customers are increasingly reserving their dollars for brands whose values they align with, so if you're known for mistreating your workers, especially marginalized workers, you'll lose customers, and also prospective hires. High-quality talent isn't going to flock to a place where it looks like everyone is running out the door, and if your organization can't attract top talent, there's most certainly a cost associated with that.

So now let's get into the more quantifiable financial repercussions of turnover—most notably, the cost of replacing an employee. According to research by Gallup, it costs one-half to two times the employee's annual salary to replace them. For a small, 20-person organization where the average salary is $50,000, assuming an average annual turnover rate of 10 percent, replacement costs could be from $50,000 to $200,000 per year. (See Figure 7)

Replacement costs

$50-200k

Left the organization

Figure 7

And it might not just be the employees feeling marginalized who are leaving (although that is bad enough!). In the fall of 2020, when Silicon Valley cryptocurrency firm Coinbase announced that it would no longer be participating in DEI and other forms of social activism, 5 percent of its workforce left. Notably, that 5 percent was *not* comprised of predominantly underrepresented workers compared to the overall workforce population. In other words, overrepresented-group workers care about DEI too. And they'll leave organizations that don't share their values for those that do. Software company Basecamp experienced this firsthand in 2021 when CEO Jason Fried announced that employees would no longer be allowed to discuss "politics, advocacy, or society at-large" at work. "That's their business, not ours," Fried wrote. "We're in the business of making software, and a few tangential things that touch that edge. We're responsible for ourselves."

Following this announcement, nearly a *third* of Basecamp's sixty employees left. Clearly DEI matters to more than just those on the fringes. While most millennials want DEI from their employers, the majority of Gen Z demands it. What companies like Basecamp and Coinbase will get with these public, anti-DEI moves is a homogenous, like-mindedness workforce—which, as research has shown, kills innovation and good decision-making.

That's the bad news. The good news is that doing DEI right can decrease an organization's turnover rate—and save the organization money. In our 20-person-company example, if the company could reduce turnover by just 5 percent, it would save up to $100,000 per year—enough to hire up to two *new* employees. (See Figure 8) And that's not counting all the money that's being saved in productivity, institutional knowledge, and reputation.

Savings

$25-100k

Stayed   Quit

Figure 8

Diversity Begets Diversity

As we've mentioned, there are key business advantages to having a more diverse workforce. More diverse groups have been shown to be more creative and innovative, and they bring with them a broader set of skills and perspectives, which are essential to problem solving. If you are swayed by research, this is a pretty compelling argument. But to business executives, increasing diversity in your workforce can sound like an uphill battle, and a costly one at that.

The truth is, it's not always easy and it's not always cheap, but a little momentum can go a long way. Diversity efforts can yield compounding results—or, as we like to say, diversity begets diversity. Basically, the more diverse an organization appears (and hopefully *is*), the more attractive it looks to candidates who share the identities of those already working there. Researchers call this a "signaling pattern." By looking at who is featured in recruitment advertisements, whose bios and photos are on the organization's website, and even who is walking into and out of the office building, potential applicants get a sense of who is getting hired—and more importantly, *staying*—at that organization. "Do I see people like me here?" is the question we all ask, consciously or subconsciously, when we are looking for a job; and if the answer is yes, we're more likely to want to work at that organization.

The ROI of Inclusion

So now you can effectively argue that it makes good business sense to invest time and money into DEI in order to attract diverse candidates and retain the people you've already hired. In fact, DEI efforts can achieve more than just costs saved by retaining more employees; the sense of belonging they gain will improve their engagement, and better engagement means higher profits. If you want to back up that claim, a meta-analysis across 276 organizations in 54 industries and 96 countries found that companies in the top quartile of engagement are 23 percent more profitable than companies in the bottom quartile.

Conversely, lower engagement means lower profits. Gallup estimated that disengagement at work costs companies up to $550 billion in lost productivity each year and that disengagement is tied to DEI. Keep in mind that people from underrepresented groups are more likely to experience workplace discrimination—an employee or job applicant's perception of unfair or biased treatment based on membership in a particular social group—which also affects engagement. A study by the Center for Talent Innovation found that employees who perceive **bias** are almost three times as likely to be disengaged at work. They're also three times as likely to be planning to leave their job within the year. On the other hand, people who show higher engagement have lower absenteeism and turnover (which we've already seen saves money!), they do higher-quality work, and the result is a 21 percent boost in profitability for their organization. Clearly, investing in DEI, especially when it comes to reducing workplace discrimination and bias, pays off.[6]

---

6   Build the case for DEI at *your* organization in our in Worksheet #3 of our Inclusalytics Workbook, available at www.inclusalytics.com/workbook

Culture Starts at the Top

By now, if you've made your case well, your organization's leaders should be able to see the value in investing in DEI work. Yet agreeing to a DEI budget and/or head count is just the first step they need to take. To make DEI efforts truly impactful, leaders need to not only be bought in but also prepared to model inclusive behaviors *and* to hold others accountable for inclusion. Why? Because an organization's culture is hugely influenced by its leadership.

Imagine being told you have to take a mandatory **unconscious bias** training (i.e., a training meant to help you identify and correct subconscious beliefs that result in discrimination against individuals from underrepresented groups). You're told it's very important for the sake of the business and that it's part of a culture-building initiative the company has prioritized. You show up to the training, and all of your coworkers are there . . . except for the head of your department. What is your impression of the importance of the training now? Are you feeling as invested as before? Just how diligent will you be about applying what you learn from the training back to your job if your leader didn't even bother showing up?

Hopefully this illustration demonstrates that until you can get senior leaders talking about DEI, enacting inclusive behaviors, and setting clear expectations of everyone in the organization, DEI work is unlikely to take hold. Therefore, leaders need to believe in the value of DEI, *and* they need to be committed to personally seeing the work through as well as role modeling inclusive leadership behaviors. Talking the talk isn't enough—they need to walk the walk and hold others accountable for doing the same.

Building in Accountability

One surefire way to ensure that leaders and supervisors remain committed to DEI is by tying DEI outcomes to their compensation. If this sounds radical or "a step too far," think of it this way: If DEI is a business imperative, then it needs to be treated as such. Other business imperatives like profitability and growth are tied to compensation, so why should DEI be any different?

Businesses are increasingly adopting this strategy. Starbucks and McDonald's provide incentives to top executives for increasing diversity in their leadership ranks. American Express and Nike have done something similar by tying a percentage of top executives' annual bonus to increasing racial and gender diversity among its workforce and managers. National Grid is another company that has successfully tied executive compensation to DEI, but only by—you guessed it—building the business case first.

"We worked really hard to create a business case, because when you work in an industry like utilities or technology or sciences, people are so focused on the productivity and outcome of the business and operations that I&D can become an add-on or an afterthought, versus being enmeshed in business case decisions," said Adam Murray, the US director of diversity, equity, and inclusion. "So that's the very first step any organization has to take: here's why we're doing this, and it's not just to be nice. There's a business reason for doing this."

In the 2022 fiscal year, National Grid will directly tie DEI metrics to compensation for its top three tiers of leadership (regional director and above). In Murray's words, "This gets people on board who might be a little resistant." But the company didn't start here. They spent several years building the business case and communicating with leadership to gain the necessary buy-in. Three years ago, their DEI team had three people. Now they have twelve. Murray also discussed how their DEI team and People Analytics teams work in tandem together to make data-driven decisions. "Both our Chief Diversity Officer and People Analytics Leader sit on our People and Culture Leadership Team." Data-driven DEI—it's music to our ears!

Getting Started

Of course, not all firms are as far along on their DEI journey as National Grid is. Let's say your organization sees DEI as a list of checkboxes—something they have to do to keep up appearances. As one DEI executive we interviewed put it, "There are still some partners, [mostly] white guys, who think clients don't really care about diversity. It's window dressing to them." Or maybe leaders simply haven't given DEI much thought but know "something has to be done."

You're going to make the business case to skeptical executives; that's without question. But there are other things you can do too. Kellie Molin Kénol, global head of diversity, equity, and inclusion at Endo International, said that she worked to obtain senior leadership buy-in by opening their eyes to the current state of affairs, even within themselves:

> *We used the IDI (Intercultural Development Inventory)[7] self-assessment to open the eyes of our leadership so that they understand where they're coming from with respect to diversity. Have they thought about it, really, in terms of their ability to be open to other cultures? The IDI assessment is great for that. I think it was really successful,*

---

7   The IDI self-assessment was developed by Hammer, Bennett, & Wiseman, 2003, and can be found at https://idiinventory.com/

because people were surprised. Some people thought, "Well, I don't see color. Isn't that a good thing? They learned through this work that colorblindness is a hinderance, not an advantage, to advancing DEI."

It's not easy, and it will take time, but obtaining executive-level buy-in is essential for DEI work to get going in any organization. We've seen this hold true for startups of fewer than ten employees, midsize nonprofits and educational institutions, and corporations of thousands. When it comes to building a more diverse, equitable, and inclusive organization, you're going to need resources, you're going to need executive-level support, and you're going to need leaders at all levels who both talk the talk *and* walk the walk. The most compelling way to do this is through data. So make the case to obtain the resources you need, and then get ready to start gathering data—and lots of it.

PART II:

"GARBAGE IN, GARBAGE OUT": GATHER DATA WORTH ANALYZING

CHAPTER 4:
Start with What You Have: Diversity Data

In today's digital-first workplace, every organization is collecting some sort of data. Yours is no exception. Whether or not you have anything remotely resembling a **DEI** function, you are collecting, at the very least, basic demographic information (diversity data!) from the people you recruit, interview, hire, onboard, develop, and offboard. This is the starting point for the data collection stage of your **Inclusalytics** journey.

Now, your organization might have a robust DEI department that is already collecting and analyzing a whole assortment of complex data—and that's great. Right now, however, we're going to look at how to build a DEI data program from the ground up. And that means starting with the basics: assessing where you are with the data you have.

INCLUSALYTICS CALLOUT

Throughout the rest of the book you'll be seeing these "Inclusalytics callouts." We really want to drive home the importance of measurement in terms of DEI. So pay special attention to these callouts!

Assess Your Current State

In the current social justice climate, when everyone wants to see action *now*, it's tempting to jump on the bandwagon of DEI interventions straightaway. After all, if society at-large is dealing with racism, sexism, and other forms of **prejudice** and **bias**, then it seems safe to assume that these issues affect every organization on the planet—in which case, diving in with a popular **unconscious bias** training program might seem like a way to show your organization cares and is making progress on the DEI front.

The thing is, applying an intervention without knowing what problem you're trying to solve is like prescribing medicine without having diagnosed the illness. Tylenol won't cure breast cancer; and if you give someone chemotherapy when they have pneumonia, you could kill them rather than cure them. This is a hyperbolic analogy, but the principle holds true: you need to figure out what DEI issues are actually affecting your organization before you go in and start trying to fix them. You need a baseline assessment.

Beyond identifying gaps, shortcomings, or outright problems, proper diagnostics will also help you identify the things your organization is also doing *well* with DEI. This is especially important in large organizations where the left hand doesn't always know what the right hand is doing. We interviewed an employee network manager who discussed that while it can be easy to get excited by initiatives you see happening at other organizations, it's important to make sure that work is not already being done somewhere within your organization. As we all know, resources for DEI work are often limited, so it would be silly to waste them reinventing the wheel!

This baseline assessment is essential when building a brand-new DEI function at an organization; however, it's equally crucial for organizations already in the thick of DEI work. The process of improving **diversity**, **equity**, and **inclusion** is cyclical; assessment is therefore never "finished." We will return to the matter of re-assessment in later chapters, but for now we're going to forge ahead as though this is the first time an organization has taken a more data-driven approach to DEI.

The HRIS Gold Mine

The vast majority of an organization's diversity data—which come primarily from demographic data—will be housed in a human resource information system (HRIS). The exact data your organization collects will depend on a number of factors (e.g., whether or not you employ 15+ or 100+ individuals or if you're a government contractor[8]), but in the United States, gender, race, and age are the most common demographic variables collected across the board. Sexual orientation is rarely, if ever, collected via HRIS; and while disability is typically collected, it is often treated as binary and generic ("Can you perform the physical requirements of this job: Yes or no?").

---

8 The U.S. Equal Employment Opportunity Commission (EEOC) requires employers with more than 100 employees to provide workforce data such as employment status by sex and race/ethnicity (lower thresholds apply to federal contractors). Employers meeting the reporting thresholds are legally obligated to provide the data; it is not voluntary. Although the data is confidential, aggregated data are available to the public (U.S. Equal Employment Opportunity Commission, n.d.).

Here is a list of possible demographics that your organization may or may not be collecting at various points in the employee life cycle:

- Gender

- Race

- Ethnicity

- Sexual orientation

- Age/generation

- Disability status

- Veteran status

- Language

- Nationality

- Degree/education level

- Residence

- Religion

- Caregiver status (to children, aging parents, those with disabilities, etc.)

This list is not exhaustive, and everything may not necessarily live in HRIS, but that system is a great first place to look for data when determining where your organization currently stands in terms of diversity. Attributes that are more "optional" to collect (although still extremely valuable), such as religion and sexual orientation, can be gathered through voluntary self-report methods such as surveys, provided you are forthcoming and transparent about why you want this information. We'll cover data-gathering best practices in Chapter 6, but the bottom line is that employees need to be able to trust that their personal information won't be used against them before they'll be willing to provide it!

Who Gets Access to DEI Data?

Now that we've pointed you in the direction of this wealth of diversity data, we must stop and address one major challenge you may encounter. It's a hurdle every external (and internal!) DEI professional must overcome to take a data-driven approach to DEI to work. The fact is, you need permission, transparency, and cooperation with those who own the data—typically HR—to be the most effective DEI leader.

Unfortunately, not every organization—or even most—will offer up easy access and cooperation when it comes to data sharing. All too often, companies bring in DEI consultants or create internal DEI roles to fix DEI problems without providing them the data they need to do their work. In fact, if the DEI role lives anywhere outside of HR, it is standard practice *not* to give that individual or team access to data due to legal and **confidentiality** concerns. Yet access to DEI data isn't just "nice to have"; it's essential. If DEI practitioners don't have access to data specific to workforce demographics, there's no way for them to accurately diagnose what DEI problems are most pressing or what interventions should be implemented to fix those problems. Going back to our medical analogy: Wouldn't you be concerned if a doctor told you they were going to operate on you or a loved one without first looking at an X-ray or MRI?

"That's been a big roadblock for us: data sharing, the integrity of the data, and understanding who's the keeper and who *should* be the keeper of the data," shared Rebecca Baumgartner. At her law firm, diversity and inclusion is its own department. Human resources doesn't share data with them, so they must collect it themselves. Adeola Oduwole, chief equity, diversity and inclusion officer at Ann & Robert H. Lurie Children's Hospital of Chicago, shared a similar struggle: "If I need data, I'm sending an email to HR to request it." This method of data-gathering is not always effective, and it's certainly not efficient.

Even if HR is agreeable and willing to share the data, their role as a go-between creates a number of challenges. First, there's the issue of delay. When one of our clients requested access to their workforce demographic data, HR took weeks to pull the data. This slowed down our momentum in building their DEI strategy because our client didn't have what they needed to make data-driven decisions about whom to target and what areas within their organization had the greatest opportunities for improvement. Once our client finally received the data, they then ran into another common issue we see with HR data: the information had been pulled in such a way that it was nearly impossible to make sense of without help from a data scientist.

At times, this frustrating DEI-HR arrangement arises out of ignorance on the part of the organization and its C-suite. Many leaders simply do not understand the importance of data when making decisions around DEI. For example, during an executive DEI workshop, we asked the executives what measures they should use to hold the leaders of their organizations accountable for DEI efforts. Crickets. When we asked the same question about holding leaders accountable for "business-related" goals, they had so many metrics to offer (e.g., labor costs, gross profit margin, cost of customer acquisition) that they were talking over each other. What they were missing was what we covered in Chapter 3: DEI *is* a business-related goal. It has very real implications for business outcomes. But until it's measured as rigorously as revenue and other business-critical performance metrics, executives will continue to write it off as a "feel-good" initiative unrelated to the core functioning, and therefore success, of the organization.

While executives' ignorance of the importance of data in DEI work is one reason HR often remains the gatekeeper, DEI data are more often kept under lock and key due to fear and risk mitigation. DEI practitioner Lindsay Ciancetta described the issue this way:

> *One of our biggest challenges in regards to leveraging data in diversity, equity, and inclusion is that by doing the real analytics, the deeper analytics, the analytics that give us meaningful insight into where we need to change and where we need to improve, we instantaneously create evidence that could be used in a court of law against the organization.*

In effect, the DEI person at an organization often can't do the job they were hired to do because the company is afraid of what will happen when DEI issues surface—which they inevitably already have. It's a big reason they handcuff outside consultants as well. "Companies can be hesitant to have somebody from the outside come in and point out what may be happening," said Terry Roberts of AEO. "It's not so much that organizations are resistant to fix issues, but more so that when they realize that there may be a hot steaming pile of you-know-what in the corner, the fix won't be easy. Even when you pick it up and throw it out, the stench might remain."

To convince HR leaders and executives to provide access to the data you need, appeal to the fact that the organization values DEI enough to have a dedicated professional (or even multiple professionals) working on it in the first place. To get ROI on those DEI budgets, you need the data necessary to do your job, do it well, and show the measured impact of your work.

Getting access to organization's data may mean going back to the C-suite and restating your case. You may need to rethink your approach if you believe the primary obstacle is fear. We will cover how to communicate DEI findings in Chapter 9, but presenting both a communications plan (e.g., who to share which findings with and when) and your approach to anonymity, confidentiality, and data protection (discussed in Chapter 6) can help.

Other Data Starting Points

So far the data we have discussed have been focused on an individual's personal identity. However, there are other role-specific pieces of data to consider as well. One example has to do with one's standing in the organization. A way to use this sort of data to judge intersections of identity and power might be to ask how many CEOs of Fortune 500 companies are women. (The pitiful answer: 8.1 percent as of 2021) Relevant "role-specific" data may include:

- Level
- Department
- Company tenure
- Time in position
- Tenure vs. nontenure
- Core vs. support staff

Then there are attributes that affect one's career progression within the organization. These start at the very beginning of the employee life cycle and extend through to the end (i.e., when an employee leaves)[9]. An example to consider from the start of an employee life cycle is how many people with disabilities, compared to those without disabilities, are applying to open roles in your organization. (These data are required by the EEOC for companies with more than 100 employees.)

Some areas to look for subgroup differences include:

- Application rates
- Selection
- Performance evaluation scores
- Promotion data
- Voluntary and involuntary turnover

Finally, there are data that are specific to a given industry. For instance, hospitals will look at demographics not only of their staff, but also of their patients and the diversity of their vendors. If the patients at a hospital are predominantly **Latiné**, how does that compare to the makeup of staff who are treating them? Organizations with a STEM focus track the number of conferences engineers and scientists attend. Are the same senior folks attending all the conferences, while

---

9   Identify data collection opportunities within *your* organization in Worksheet #4 of our Inclusalytics Workbook, available at www.inclusalytics.com/workbook

more junior scientists are left behind? Are they sending mostly white "manels" (male-only conference panels) or are they sending women—and especially women of color—as well? Law firms evaluate the composition of their pitch teams as well as their work teams—if they win the business. Who is getting selected for these teams, and who is commonly left out?

In the modern era, organizations are awash in data. Therefore, our Inclusalytics journey begins with figuring out what metrics are already available. Most of these data contribute to the "diversity" side of DEI, and a lot can be learned from them! But not everything can be derived from demographics, especially when it comes to who has/does not have access to power and resources within an organization . . . which is why we're gathering equity data next.

CHAPTER 5:
Conduct an Equity Audit

Once you've gathered as much **diversity** data as you can (or, more likely, *while* you're collecting that data), it's time to move on to collecting equity data. If diversity data have to do with individuals—who they are and the various identity groups to which they belong—then equity data is about the organizational policies, practices, and procedures that, in a sense, "govern" those individuals.

Equity is the distribution of power and resources across an organization. In a word, it's referring to the *fairness* of how an organization operates. Do groups with different levels of underlying social advantage/disadvantage—e.g., wealth, power, or prestige—receive equal treatment? (Note that we didn't use the word "access," as in "equal access to power and resources." Equal access is important, but access alone won't necessarily right an equity imbalance.)

When trying to understand or explain the "E" in "**DEI**," we find it helpful to think of equity in terms of **Targeted Universalism**. Targeted Universalism, a concept popularized by john powell, a professor of law and African American Studies at UC Berkeley, gets at the necessity of having both an overarching goal that involves everyone—building more diverse, equitable, and inclusive organizations—and taking targeted approaches to meeting the unique needs of specific populations within that broader community. It's not one or the other—you need both.

We're first introduced to the concept of Targeted Universalism by Gina Winstead, assistant vice president at Vibrant Pittsburgh, a Pittsburgh-based nonprofit where the mission is to build a thriving and inclusive region by attracting, retaining, and elevating a diversity of talent.

When we work with companies who want to build and implement more DEI-focused practices, Targeted Universalism goes hand in hand with ensuring those practices are equitable. We ask, 'What are the decisions that you are making as an organization that are targeted to the specific populations you want to attract and retain?' Companies may think that broad (i.e., universal) DEI practices would appeal to women and members of the LBGTQ+ community and Black and Brown employees. But that's not enough. The practice has to take into consideration who the people are and what their barriers are.

Imagine you're doing DEI work within a school district. A universal goal may be that everyone is graduating high school, that you have a very low attrition rate. For specific communities, the 'targeted' part would be recognizing that there is a disparity for Black students graduating and that disparity comes from identifying the root cause and then solving for that root cause.

Extending Winstead's example, imagine you then identified that one root cause of the higher attrition rate of Black students is that this population is less likely to have access to home internet, so they cannot do many of their homework assignments, or access remote learning opportunities. A targeted practice—and therefore equitable—would be to develop a program that provides internet hotspots with a focus on outreach explicitly to Black families.

Pay equity is perhaps the most common example of an equity issue. It's both a literal resource and also a secondary indicator of power within an organization—those who are paid more tend to be granted more power. It's a popular metric because, as we showed in Chapter 2, it is fairly easy to understand and measure. Compensation data can easily be found in an HRIS (human resource information system). Moreover, from a logistical standpoint (i.e., putting aside where the budget would come from), those numbers can be changed fairly quickly and easily. The tricky part is uncovering formal and informal determinants of who makes what to figure out if inequities exist between different groups.

The fact that many policies, practices, and procedures possess both objective (hard, undisputable numbers) and subjective (open to interpretation) components is what makes equity so challenging to measure. Finding the rules that prescribe salary tiers is easy; figuring out how and why these rules were created, how they are enforced, and how people feel about them is less so. Therefore, an **equity audit**—the shorthand term for evaluating equity within an organization—needs to include both objective and subjective measures.

The Power of Perception

Every equity audit should begin with subjective data, or perceptions. What workers think and feel about fairness within your organization will point you toward areas that may need to be examined more closely for sources of inequity.

To gauge general equity sentiment across the organization, you can include items within an **engagement** or **pulse survey** like, "Policies are designed to support employees from all diverse backgrounds." If you have space for more focused items or the ability to conduct a separate DEI survey, the three key areas of equity to investigate are perceived fairness, distribution of resources, and decision-making. Some example items include:

- Perceived fairness item: my job performance is evaluated fairly.

- Distribution of resources item: people from all backgrounds have equal opportunities to succeed at this organization.

- Decision-making item: I am included in decisions that affect my work.

Finally, you can ask targeted questions about areas that tend to be perceived as inequitable within organizations generally or where you suspect inequity may be an issue within your organization specifically. You'll especially want to do this if you've already collected objective data that indicate there might be a problem in a certain area.

In addition to what people are paid, some other areas to explore for potential perceived inequities are:

- Organization mission and vision (Who is your organization serving? Are their voices being centered?)

- Recruitment (Who is being recruited? Where are they being recruited from? Who is doing the recruiting?)

- Hiring policies (Is the interviewing process standardized? Who conducts the interviews?)

- Selection (Who is doing the selecting? Who is being selected?)

- Performance reviews (Who conducts them? Have they been trained to look out for potential **bias**? Is the process serving everyone equally?)

- Professional development plans (How are these drafted? Who is responsible for progress being made?)

- Paid family leave (Is it offered? Who takes it and who doesn't? What are the rules governing its use?)

- Flex time/work from home (Who are formal policies serving? Do informal practices support or undermine the formal policies?)

As an example, an issue that we are seeing arise with increasing frequency largely due to the COVID-19 pandemic is how organizations are enforcing their hybrid/work-from-home policies. Often, a flexible work-from-home policy is only as flexible as the managers enforcing it. If there's one policy on paper and another in practice, that's likely to result in inequity, because ir*regular* enforcement inevitably becomes in*equitable* enforcement. Yet you won't know this is happening until you ask the employees who are being affected—and, more often than not, these are employees whose voices often go unheard on numerous matters, not just this one.

You can ask equity-related questions of the entire workforce via engagement or DEI surveys. However, it's especially important to also ask them in **focus groups** or **employee resource groups** (each of which is discussed in greater detail in Chapters 7 and 12, respectively) because marginalized groups often feel safer and more willing to voice their true opinions in those forums. Ask what policies or practices are serving underrepresented employees well. Which are frustrating? Are any perceived as harmful and/or prevent them from reaching their full potential at the organization?

Now be prepared: leaders will hear employee feedback and respond with, "They said we don't promote or pay equally, but they don't know what everyone's making or why someone was promoted." These leaders have a point—*perceived* inequity does not always indicate that something is inequitable. But workers' perceptions don't exist in a vacuum. That's why we start equity audits with perceptions. How employees think and feel about organizational practices, policies, and procedures will help you best direct your equity-building efforts into what matters most to your current workforce. Sometimes, the solution can be as simple as dispelling myths (e.g., people falsely believing that new dads are taking a ton of paid time off, when in reality dads either don't know about paternity leave or are choosing not to take it). Other times, though, you'll have to dig deeper to uncover why some workers feel like they don't have the same amount of resources and power as others. Digging into these perceptions may cause you to find that there really *is* an issue with a particular policy. It can require looking through a new lens to see inequity clearly—and then, armed with this new data, you can take the appropriate action to fix it.

Beyond the Current Workforce

Because inequities can—and do—exist anywhere in the workforce lifecycle, don't just ask your *current* workforce what they think; ask people in your current **talent pipeline**, including those who have self-selected out, about their experiences with recruitment and hiring. Ask individuals who leave the organization about what they encountered and whether there were any structures or practices that were problematic.

Collecting this data doesn't need to be complicated. Exit interview or follow-up survey questions can be as basic as:

What were the reasons you turned down the job offer?

Did any policies negatively impact your employee experience?

Why did you leave this organization?

You can also ask the broader community in which you are operating about their perceptions of your organization: What do your customers think of your organization? Do your vendors see your practices as equitable? Are shareholders satisfied with how your employees are treated? Asking these questions and digging into their answers with follow-up questions will give you guidance on where to focus further data collection efforts inside the organization. (Plus, when customers and vendors perceive that an organization treats its people fairly, they're often more willing to buy from and/or work with that organization. It really does influence the bottom line!)

Policies, Practices, and Procedures

While your workforce and community are providing their feedback, your next task is to identify all of the practices, policies, and procedures your organization has in place. DEI practitioner Lindsay Ciancetta said that "When it comes to equity, that's when I want to look at every single talent process within an organization." This is also where gathering objective data comes in. Before deciding which policy should be updated to reduce inequity, for instance, you need to first assess which groups are potentially being left behind as a result of that policy.

Here are some common areas where equity issues arise:

- *Recruitment*—Is every applicant screened using the same criteria? Are any job specifications unnecessarily screening out certain applicants (e.g., education requirements precluding low-SES **BIPOC** applicants, ableist requirements precluding disabled applicants)?

- *Hiring*—How many people are on hiring panels? (A hiring panel of only one or two individuals will be skewed toward their biases.) Are the panels representative of a broad range of identities?

- *Development and Advancement*—Who decides which individuals are eligible for education and training opportunities? Is there a formal selection process in place? How are promotions decided and by whom? Do you publicly promote these resources to all employees?

- *Benefits*—Who has access to particular benefits and who is excluded? An example is health insurance: Are partners in same-sex and/or unmarried couples eligible? Does your organization's health insurance cover providers and procedures LGBTQ+ individuals may need?

- *Time off*—Is time off dictated by a particular group's religious practices? Are individuals with chronic pain or mental illness forced to take their sick days out of their vacation time?

- *Pregnancy and childbirth*—What accommodations are (or are not) made for expectant mothers? What about nursing mothers? How much paid time off do new parents get, and is the policy applicable to nonbirthing parents (including those who foster or adopt)? Does the leave policy apply to the entire workforce or only corporate or salaried staff?

- *Accommodations and access*—What requirements exist to ensure physical spaces and digital products are both accessible to and usable by employees with disabilities? Are your communication channels utilized to better accommodate people who are neurodivergent? (A *lack* of a policy or procedure can create inequity too.)

Identifying Inequities

If no one is overtly complaining about a particular practice, policy, or procedure (or, more likely, if you just aren't *hearing* complaints), it can be tricky to identify which are most problematic. This is where peer-to-peer comparison can come in handy.

One especially useful source of comparison is indices that aggregate data from organizations within a sector, like technology. One example is the Race Equ(al)ity Index, developed by the Race Equ(al)ity Project. Its goal is to create a benchmark for tech companies in the following areas: benefits and education, recruiting and talent management, **representation**, inclusive design practice, learning, employee resource groups, the DEI department, and public statements.

Similar indices exist for women (Gender-Equality Index), people with disabilities (Disability Equality Index), and LGBTQ+ employees (Human Rights Campaign). Collectively, the purpose of these indices is to allow participating companies to see how they rank against one another and against a particular industry at-large in order to identify areas for improvement.

Another useful source of data is the Equal Employment Opportunity (EEO) Census Tabulation. These census data capture individuals who are qualified and available in the external labor market, giving organizations a sense of "what's out there" and whether their workforce accurately reflects the existing talent pool. These data are particularly useful to federal contractors completing annual affirmative action program requirements by helping them to set appropriate hiring and retention benchmarks for women and/or historically disadvantaged groups. However, the data can also be used by organizations who do not have legal requirements to meet but simply want a representative workforce.

Who is Being Hurt, Who Can Be Helped

Once you've identified equity issues, it's time to see whom they affect. As you review your survey data, look at who gave what answer and whether there are any observable trends across subgroups (e.g., gender, race, disability, veteran status, etc.). You can also check to see who is actually using a given policy and who is not. Going back to our earlier work-from-home example: if one group is predominantly working from home or if a certain group *never* works from home, that's a red flag that either the policy is inequitable or its implementation is causing inequity. For example, those who never work from home may be more likely to get selected for more high profile (read: promotion-worthy) not because they're necessarily better for the role, but simply because they're physically present and therefore top of mind.

Another thing you can do is work backward from an unwelcome outcome to identify practices or policies that may be causing it.[10] Let's say your organization operates in a community with a large Asian population, but you aren't getting a representative number of Asian hires. When you look into your recruiting and hiring processes, you don't find any policy issue that would be off-putting to these applicants, but you *do* discover a procedural data integrity issue: there is no consistent, reliable, timely way of tracking outcomes from your applicant flow process. How do you know if the hiring manager reviewed an applicant's resume? Are they unknowingly passing up resumes with Asian-sounding names due to some sort of **unconscious bias**? Is the applicant always matched with the most fitting job? Did the recruiter gauge the candidate's interest before proceeding? Who got an interview and who didn't? These are all practices that, if skipped—and particularly if they're skipped for *specific candidates* (in this case, Asian candidates)—can result in inequitable hiring practices.

---

10   Explore how *your* organization's policies, practices, and procedures may benefit or disadvantage certain groups in Worksheet #5 of our Inclusalytics Workbook, available at www.inclusalytics. com/workbook

Seek the Origin Story

Finally, as you examine your organization's existing policies, practices, and procedures, it's important to understand where they originated. Why did your organization—or, taking an even broader view, your industry—establish these norms? Who established them and what purposes did they serve?

"We need to spend more time understanding where things came from in preparation for the future," said Amber Thompson. An equity and inclusion consultant herself, Thompson is also the founder of de-bias, a digital platform that connects business outcomes to social issues through data accountability by enabling all stakeholders to anonymously share grievances about a business that employers can then use to identify and solve inequities.

"Everything was born out of some sort of oppression," she says. Therefore, before an organization can make any useful changes, it's necessary to understand how a policy, practice, or procedure was developed to oppress N or suppress (certain) people. The questions to ask are: How was this used in the past to prevent certain groups from attaining money, **privilege**, or power? How has it changed? What barriers does it still present to these (or other) groups?

Understanding the history behind organizational structures is an important part of uncovering DEI blind spots. We want to find and solve problems that are "here and now" because, as we all know, you can't change the past. However, the past informs the present. So while will we spend the rest of this book talking about what to do to move forward with "new" data you have collected, remember to always look into the history behind anything you are attempting to change. The more you learn about a structure's oppressive origins, the better position you'll be in to disrupt them.

CHAPTER 6:

Collect Quantitative Data
(the "What" of Workplace Inclusion)

We've come to the third and final category of **DEI** data: **inclusion** data. Collecting this type of data is often an effortful and resource-intensive process, but it's absolutely crucial, because inclusion data are what give meaning to **diversity** data. To illustrate: If your diversity data tell you there are only two boomers in a department full of millennials, that might seem like an issue. However, if those boomers feel that they belong—that is, if they feel their authentic selves are valued, respected, seen, and heard—then your DEI resources may be better spent elsewhere. You can't know whether or not the boomers are feeling included unless you gather data—from them!—so that's what this chapter is all about.

There are a number of ways to categorize inclusion data. One way is as *leading* versus *lagging* measures. Leading measures are forward looking, and they change quickly. They are seen as signposts indicating how a sentiment or activity is progressing (or stalling) and therefore can help determine where you should focus (or pivot) your DEI efforts. Examples are survey responses regarding people's perceptions of current DEI initiatives or how likely people are to use the behaviors they learned in a DEI training. Other leading measures could be nonsurvey metrics like managers' completion rates of **unconscious bias** training or the number of people participating in DEI events.

Whereas leading indicators look ahead, lagging indicators look backward. They measure performance data that were already captured and tell you whether or not you have made progress toward your desired outcomes. These indicators are often viewed as more hard-and-fast data, like workforce demographic trends in new hires, retention, and who is promoted. But they can also be things like **engagement** data gathered from company-wide surveys, sliced by demographic groups.

We'll be examining both leading and lagging indicators in the next two chapters, but we're going to use two different categories to organize them: **quantitative data** and **qualitative data**.

Quantitative data deals with "quantity"—that is, it has to do with numbers.[11] Think averages, medians, modes, percentages, frequencies, and other advanced statistics. . . . If it can be measured and expressed numerically, it's quantitative data. As such, when you're collecting quantitative data, you must know what each number represents. You can't count a thing if you don't know what you're counting! This is why the common DEI phrase of "moving the needle" makes us roll our eyes when there aren't hard numbers associated with it.

Determining "what numbers represent" is formally called **operationalizing** data. First, you must define what you intend to measure—your construct—in terms of what it is and what it is not. Take Fahrenheit: It measures temperature, often how hot or cold it is outside. It does not measure other elements of weather such as humidity or wind speed. In order for Fahrenheit to be useful, it must always measure temperature; we cannot change the definition one day to measuring precipitation! The same goes for DEI constructs like inclusion: once a definition has been assigned, this definition must be used consistently for that construct to remain useful. This is why we're sticklers about operationalizing inclusion as the *behaviors* that make others feel valued, respected, seen, and heard. By operationalizing inclusion as behaviors, we can see and measure whether inclusive behaviors are being utilized. Then we can choose interventions to increase certain behaviors that may currently be underutilized according to the data.

The second step in operationalizing data is to create a consistent scale for measuring your construct. Fahrenheit is measured numerically, with lower numbers indicating colder temperatures and higher numbers indicating hotter temperatures. The same rigor must be brought to DEI measurements. As a rule, higher numbers should always indicate "more" of whatever is being measured. Thus, if a survey item is measuring inclusive behaviors and using a 4-point scale, the 1 would indicate a low measurement (e.g., "not at all" or "rarely"), and the 4 would indicate a high measurement (e.g., "a great deal" or "always").

Few businesspeople are trained in creating these sorts of valid, reliable scales—in fact, there's a whole scientific field called **psychometrics** that is dedicated to the creation and study of valid, useful measurement tools like surveys. It's also why we're in business: we specialize in turning abstract concepts like **belonging** and inclusive leadership into quantifiable metrics. Therefore, you won't be surprised to hear us say that this is a point in the DEI process where partnering with an **industrial-organizational (I-O) psychologist** (you may even already have one in-house!) can be advantageous, especially when it comes to building and implementing employee surveys.

---

11 Begin turning inclusion into hard numbers at *your* organization by completing Worksheet #6 of the Inclusalytics Workbook, available at www.inclusalytics.com/workbook

Surveys

Surveys are arguably the number one tool for collecting inclusion data, and here's why: most organizations already conduct some version of an engagement survey at least once a year. Engagement surveys are a tool for assessing and beginning to change workplace behaviors, as well as for making employees feel heard. Employees are already accustomed to filling out engagement surveys annually (sometimes with **pulse surveys** in between), so it shouldn't be hard to add a few DEI questions, also called "items," such as the sample **equity** items we discussed in Chapter 5.

In an ideal situation, an organization will also have a separate DEI survey that goes out annually to enable a deeper analysis of specific items and subscales. There can be other surveys too—for instance, in-person exit interviews are increasingly being supplemented by exit surveys. Also, we're beginning to see more inclusive behaviors included in 360 surveys, commonly used in performance evaluation processes. Suffice to say, there are many opportunities for surveying your workforce about inclusion!

Whether you're adding a few items to an existing survey or sending out a survey dedicated entirely to DEI, the general inclusion categories you want to measure are inclusive behaviors and feelings of belongingness. As a reminder, we define inclusion as the *behaviors* that make others feel valued, respected, seen, and heard. How often someone utilizes inclusive behaviors shouldn't be assessed by that person themself, but rather by others who interact with that individual. Therefore, raters should indicate how frequently their peers, direct supervisors, and leaders use inclusive behaviors. Some sample survey items include:

- Senior leaders openly discuss the importance of DEI.
- My coworkers at my organization treat me with respect.
- My supervisor makes me feel heard.

Belongingness, as we discussed in Chapter 2, is the feeling that one's authentic self is valued, respected, seen, and heard. The important thing to emphasize in this construct is that it's a *feeling*—It is measuring how someone feels rather than how they behave (which is what the construct of inclusion measures). Here are a few examples of survey items that would measure belonging:

- I can be my authentic self at work.
- I feel valued at work.

It's worth noting that while survey items can, in theory, measure inclusive behaviors and belongingness separately, people's responses to these items will often be correlated, or closely linked to other constructs like engagement and

commitment. As a reminder, engagement is the mental and emotional connection employees feel toward their workplace, the people they work with, and the work they do. (An example survey item might be, "I feel like I do meaningful work.") Commitment is an employee's personal feeling of responsibility toward their organization and the people with whom they work. (Example survey item: "I see myself working at this company three years from now.")

As Rebecca Baumgartner, senior diversity and inclusion manager at a global labor and employment law firm, told us, "The more people feel like they belong, the more they feel welcomed, the more engaged they are, the more you have an understanding of the inclusive culture you have built." In other words, employees who score high on belongingness are likely to also feel very engaged and committed . . . but the inverse is not always true, which is why including survey items to measure each variable separately is so important.

Creating Survey Items

If you're going to launch a survey that includes DEI items, you must first decide what those items will be. Particularly if you are adding items to an existing survey, you shouldn't add many more and make the survey unreasonably long; so it's crucial to get the most out of the items you choose. We highly recommend that if you're going to have somebody build survey items, run the analyses, and interpret them, it should be someone with training in psychometrics, statistics, survey design and administration, and data management. This might sound self-interested, since we as I-O psychologists have this training, but the repercussions of doing this wrong are pretty serious. At best you'll gather data that turn out to be useless; at worst you'll turn people against DEI work because the conclusions you have drawn are not only wrong but risk further marginalizing already underrepresented or historically disadvantaged individuals and groups.

Whether you hire an external consultant or team up with an internal survey expert, it's important to understand what goes into strong survey items. The key is to focus on the insights you are seeking and make sure each item answers a specific question you have. For instance, let's say you're trying to figure out whether your company culture is inclusive. It's not enough to determine how frequently people are demonstrating inclusive behaviors; you need to also determine how strongly people feel that they are valued, respected, seen, and heard by others—especially those from underrepresented groups.

To make this idea more tangible, we're going to walk through how to improve an inclusion survey item step by step. Here's a survey item one may ask to assess inclusive leadership:

Version 1: "I believe I am an inclusive leader."

Strongly Disagree = 1, Disagree = 2, Agree = 3, Strongly Agree = 4

There are several issues with this question, but the first and most glaring one is that it's asking what someone believes about their own behaviors. Beliefs are fine when it comes to measuring feelings that are *outcomes* of inclusion (i.e., belonging). However, when it comes to measuring behaviors, self-reported beliefs are subjective, unobservable, and inconsistent—all qualities you do not want when designing a valid and reliable survey. On the other hand, asking about the enactment of specific behaviors themselves (not beliefs about generalized behavior) will make the measurement more objective, observable, and reliable.

Keeping in mind that in this example we want to measure inclusion, which is about *behaviors* (not beliefs), we'll attempt to improve the original survey item by updating it to:

Version 2: "I create an inclusive environment in our team."

Strongly Disagree = 1, Disagree = 2, Agree = 3, Strongly Agree = 4

Believe it or not, this item is actually still asking about beliefs. The rating scale is causing the problem: agreement and disagreement are beliefs; they're not objective. By changing the rating scale to one measuring *frequency*, we can adapt the question to ask about objective, observable behaviors:

Version 3: "I create an inclusive environment in our team."

Never = 1, Sometimes = 2, Usually = 3, Always = 4

This is a better item, but still not great. The reason is that when assessing inclusion, the feedback needs to come from the *recipients* of the inclusive behaviors, not those performing them. This goes back to the insights you are trying to gain: Are you concerned with whether people are enacting inclusive behaviors or whether the targets of those behaviors experience feelings of belonging as a result? Put another way: only the receiving end of inclusive behaviors matters. It can be interesting to measure the inclusive behaviors the managers are trying to perform and compare that against how included their reports feel, but at the end of the day, the managers' intentions don't matter to the desired outcome; if their behaviors aren't *perceived* as inclusive, then your company is not fostering a culture of inclusion.

To further improve the survey item, we'll update it so that it's asking the recipient—the employee—about the manager, rather than asking the manager about themselves:

Version 4: "My manager makes me feel included on my team."

Never = 1, Sometimes = 2, Usually = 3, Always = 4

Now we're getting closer. This item asks about observable actions, it assesses the frequency of those actions (rather than beliefs about them), and it has the person taking the survey rate someone other than themselves. But what does the word "included" mean? And, more importantly, will everyone taking the survey interpret that word the same way? It's possible, but it's not likely.

As we've discussed several times now, inclusive behaviors lead to feelings of belonging: feeling valued, respected, seen, and heard. By incorporating elements of belonging into our survey item, we can more concretely define how we want people to interpret "feeling included":

Version 5: "My manager makes sure my voice is heard in meetings."

Never = 1, Sometimes = 2, Usually = 3, Always = 4

At last, we have a great DEI survey question!

Validity, Reliability, and Verification

An excellent survey question is one thing, but to effectively measure a phenomenon like inclusion and its change over time, the item—indeed the whole survey—needs to have more qualities: it needs to be valid, it needs to be reliable, and the data it collects need to be verified.

In the context of psychometrics, the terms "**validity**" and "**reliability**" have very specific meanings.

Validity essentially means that an item measures what it's designed to measure. A validated survey item predicts something across time and across people, and it predicts outcomes or correlates to some other phenomena strongly and consistently. For instance, let's say you administer a DEI survey that asks about turnover intentions of underrepresented groups, and the results correlate highly with objective turnover data pulled from the organization's human resource information system (HRIS). That's half of the evidence you need to show that your survey is valid; the correlation then needs to last over time and across different individuals and groups to be considered "valid."

Besides being valid, your survey needs to be *reliable*. This means that it not only needs to measure what you intend for it to measure, but that it measures that thing consistently. Think of a wristwatch: A watch is a valid measurement tool because it was designed to tell the time, and it does that job well (when you look at a watch, you can see that the time is 4:05 or 8:47). However, for a watch to be reliable, that time must be consistently accurate. Is the watch fast some days and slow other days? If so, it's not reliable. The same goes for survey items.

Finally, there's the matter of verifying the data that these valid, reliable survey items are collecting. **Verification** is the process of checking, confirming, making sure, and being certain of the results of your assessment. In other words, is what you think you're finding actually what you're finding? Have you uncovered all there is to be found about it?

While it sounds like verifying your data would be something you do after you collect it, verification strategies actually need to be built into the data collection process. The primary strategy is called **triangulation**: using multiple methods and data sources to study the same thing. This could look like asking about something such as belonging on a survey and then asking again in **focus groups** to ensure the results align. This is one of the reasons we emphasize using both quantitative and qualitative data collection—otherwise known as "mixed methods"—in DEI work. Both are necessary to get the full picture!

Beware of Survey Fatigue

Once you've developed a whole bunch of reliable, validated survey items, it can be tempting to deploy them all. After all, when it comes to DEI, there is so much to measure! Unfortunately, sending frequent and/or lengthy surveys will actually thwart your data-gathering efforts, for one primary reason: **survey fatigue**.

Survey fatigue is what happens when your audience (in this case your employees) becomes bored by, uninterested in, or annoyed by your surveys. If you bog down your workers with too many surveys, they'll stop filling them out, and then you'll have *no* employee voice data. Alternatively, if you send out a survey only once or twice a year but that survey has three hundred items on it, the survey taker is likely to give up midway (again depriving you of data) or to rush through to the end (giving you inaccurate data, which is arguably worse than no data at all).

Some industries, like the legal profession, are more vulnerable to survey fatigue than others. In fact, we heard the same complaint from every DEI leader in a law firm that we interviewed: too many surveys! Still, no matter your industry, the overarching issue is the same: if you want to get robust, accurate data, you need to find the sweet spot between surveying your workers too often and surveying them so infrequently that the survey becomes unbearably long. On average, a person can complete three to five questions per minute. If you are targeting a fifteen-minute survey, which is the maximum length we recommend, you should aim for forty-five to seventy-five items. However, it is important to note that open-ended questions may extend this time, so factor that in as you design your survey.

Other Quantitative Data Collection Tools

A viable solution to survey fatigue is to collect the quantitative data you want in ways other than traditional surveys, which are usually sent out by email, with a link to a virtual landing page, etc. One way to do this is with a tool like AllieBot,[12] or "Allie," which we use with some of our clients. Allie is a chatbot integrated with the messaging app Slack and has a number of features, several of which are intervention-oriented, which we'll discuss in Chapter 12. In the context of data gathering, AllieBot's key feature is the ability to automatically administer pulse surveys.

Pulse surveys are short micro-surveys deployed at regular intervals or following a particular action that an individual has performed (e.g., attended a DEI training). They offer an easy way to ask employees questions in a less disruptive, less time-consuming way than traditional surveys, and administering them through a familiar messaging app like Slack helps them to become just another part of an employee's regular workday. According to founder and CEO of Allie, Emilie Hsieh:

> *Customers have 20 to 40 percent higher survey completion rates compared to traditional survey tools. Because employees can respond directly in Slack, they are more likely to respond versus having to log into another platform. DEI leaders can launch pulse surveys to gauge DEI sentiment immediately, rather than the traditional process of negotiating with the broader HR and data teams to add a few DEI items to an annual employee engagement survey.*

Another **Inclusalytics** partner of ours, Rhabit,[13] is reimagining the annual performance review process by breaking it into a weekly, sixty-second exercise that combines employee feedback with quick swipe technology. Rhabit requires minimal time or commitment: by having fellow employees rate one another on their weekly use of inclusive behaviors, this tool can be used to help foster inclusive behaviors across a workforce by collecting and reporting this data at the individual, team, and organizational levels. According to Rhabit's co-founder and chief science officer, Alexander Schwall:

---

12   Learn more about Allie at https://www.alliebot.com/

13   Learn more about Rhabit at https://www.rhabitanalytics.com/

For DEI to mean anything, it needs to be consistently reflected in employees' and leaders' behaviors. It is not enough to print your inclusive values on your website and water bottles—they need to be demonstrated every day. Rhabit allows companies to measure and quantify key behaviors that reflect an organization's vision, mission, and values, especially when it comes to fostering workplace inclusion.

Some data collection tools require no additional employee time or input at all. One such tool is MindStand. Using artificial intelligence (AI), MindStand scrapes email, messenger apps, and other employee communication platforms to identify trends and anomalies that can foster or thwart inclusivity. MindStand's CEO, Michael Ogunsanya, shared that, "When responding to questions about inclusion, often [a company's] solution is to 'build a great culture.' But culture change is very complicated and nuanced—specific to each individual organization and even teams. MindStand accounts for the nuance that happens in day-to-day operations and communication by pulling and integrating data from a variety of sources." The tool does this by measuring inclusive language (or lack thereof) in corporate communications, capturing discriminatory and exclusionary language across various internal communication platforms (think email or Slack), and identifying high-performing teams and how they communicate with one another, to name just a few examples.

Finally, as useful as these tools are, you don't always need *new* tools to collect data through nonsurvey means; many of the apps and programs organizations already use collect plenty of data. For instance, Outlook and Google can reveal answers to questions like who is regularly being invited to meetings and who is not; who is being copied on emails and who is being left out; who is RSVPing to DEI events and who is not. The answers to all of these questions are sources of objective, quantifiable inclusion data. You just need to be intentional with how you pull and use it to effectively measure variables important to your DEI efforts.

"What's in It for Me?"

Regardless of what data collection tools you select, there's the not-so-small matter of incentivizing people—*all* people—to use them. Some people love to take surveys and share their opinions generously. But that's not true of everyone. Therefore, it's up to the organization to come up with ways to motivate people to participate in data collection.

One option is to tie participation to compensation—á la, "If you want your bonus, you'll make sure your reports fill out our survey." The problem with this method is twofold. First, making a survey mandatory reduces feelings of **confidentiality**, no matter what the reality is. Second, it risks people gaming the system and clicking through the survey as fast as they can without putting any thought into their answers. For these reasons, we strongly discourage using this approach.

It's far better, but certainly more challenging, to try and internally motivate participation by tying it to what is valued in the company culture. Emphasizing teamwork and "Your participation will contribute to the collective good" are good strategies. Also, tell them what the point of the survey is and how the data will be used! Share the value proposition behind what you are trying to learn and what you intend to do with those learnings. Being transparent can go a long way toward obtaining employees' cooperation, buy-in, and engagement. Be sure to follow through by sharing survey findings and next steps with your workforce, which we discuss in detail in Chapter 9.

Additionally, don't disregard the power of **nudges**. Sending reminder emails to complete a survey or sign up for a focus group can be very effective, especially if you capitalize on peer pressure. As soon as your survey response rate hits 51 percent, communicate this fact to the nonresponders. "The majority of your colleagues have participated; don't miss this chance to have your voice heard!" Hearing that so many of their coworkers have already spoken up can be a compelling message.

Confidentiality, Anonymity, Honesty . . . Oh My!

All the incentives in the world won't get you the data you need if people are concerned about retaliation. People often worry that their answers will be traced back to them and that if they say something unpopular or something someone with more power and authority doesn't like, they'll be punished. In other words, they're worried about confidentiality.

Confidentiality means keeping information secret or private, but the receiver of the information (e.g., your data analyst) knows where the information came from. Be careful not to confuse this with *anonymity*, which means the information is completely unidentified, even from your data analyst. In a focus group (which we'll discuss in the next chapter), the facilitator can reassure the participants that whatever they share will be kept confidential; however, because everyone in a focus group meets face-to-face, it is near impossible for participants to remain **anonymous**.

Surveys, on the other hand, can collect information confidentially or anonymously. Our preference is to keep respondents' information confidential rather than anonymous. When surveys are conducted this way, individual survey links are sent to each respondent, which enables us to track who has completed the survey and who has not, which is valuable information in and of itself. That way, we can send out targeted messages to those who haven't yet completed the survey without spamming those who have. When the survey window closes, we strip out all identifying data before encrypting what remains and storing it on our secure servers for analysis.

There are several benefits to going the confidential route. Because this method gives us the ability to prepopulate the survey with demographic data an organization has about its employees, the survey is shorter (since we don't have to ask respondents to fill out those questions), missing data is reduced (because again, there are fewer fields to fill in), and there is less chance of error (e.g., a man accidentally saying he's a woman). Furthermore, the possibility of "ballot stuffing" or duplicate survey entries by the same person is eliminated because each person has a unique survey link that closes once that survey is completed.

The downside to this method is that participants remain linked to their responses before we strip identifying data from the files. Participants know this, and it can make them nervous about responding honestly. However, we've found that when we reassure them that the data are kept confidential and will only be reported at the aggregate (i.e., group) level, their fears often subside. Moreover, having a third-party provider issue the survey adds a measure of confidence: if we are administering a survey for an organization, only *we* have access to the employees' raw data, not the employer. It's our job to protect respondents' identities, and we have no stake in identifying and punishing those who have less-than-positive things to say about DEI at their organization. So there's no reason not to be honest!

— INCLUSALYTICS CALLOUT ——————————

To further protect confidentiality, we recommend a requirement of at least three responses to be received for a group before you can report out any findings. For instance, if there is only one Asian woman in your company and you report her responses, it will be identifiable to the entire organization even though she isn't named. However, her results could still be included in other groups that do meet the minimum requirement of three responses and the overall results.

Alternatively, conducting a survey anonymously involves sending a single survey link to all respondents, with no ability to track who has or has not completed the survey. The benefit to doing it this way is that respondents are assured of complete anonymity; their responses cannot be traced back to them. However, this method has a number of drawbacks. For one thing, reminders to complete the survey will be sent to everyone—a real annoyance to those who already submitted their responses. The survey will be longer because of the need for questions collecting all of the demographic data that the confidential method would have prepopulated. People might make mistakes when entering their demographic data, resulting in all of their answers being analyzed as part of the wrong group. And finally, people can "ballot stuff," or complete the survey more than once, skewing results.

Quantitative Data is Not Infallible

Hopefully by now you can see that as much as we like numbers (and we really do), quantitative data alone is insufficient. Not everything can be reduced to a ratio or a percentage. Statistics can't tell you the nuanced experiences of people, and they certainly can't tell you how to *change* those experiences.

We point this out because we have found that business leaders, like many scientists, tend to lean heavily on quantitative data—sometimes to a fault. The issue is that oftentimes in research (and in life), you don't know what you don't know. We like to say that the quantitative data is the "what," while the qualitative data is the "why." The "what" cannot tell the whole story! That's why the best DEI approaches incorporate a mixture of quantitative *and* qualitative data.

CHAPTER 7:
Collect Qualitative Data
(the "Why" of Workplace Inclusion)

If you're dealing with humans and you want to understand (and maybe change) mindsets and behaviors, you need more than **quantitative data**; you need **qualitative data**. Here's an example we heard from one of our interviewees: Based on employee retention data (quantitative data!) their firm was collecting, they began to notice that they were losing a high proportion of Black associates who had been with the firm for three to six years. Digging deeper into the data, they found that these associates were leaving because they had low billable hours. The business problem was now clear—but the causes of the problem, and therefore how to solve it, were not. It was not until the firm spoke to some of their Black associates in interviews and **focus groups**, thereby collecting qualitative data, that they uncovered why their billable hours were so low: the associates were struggling to make connections across the firm and, as a result, were struggling to land new clients. Without landing new clients, they couldn't increase their billable hours, which was negatively affecting their overall **commitment** to and long-term success at the firm.

With this human-centric "why" data, the firm could find solutions to the problem of losing so many Black midcareer associates. They established a program that partnered these associates with successful senior- or executive-level leaders to work on a career development plan, introduce them to new clients, find opportunities to increase their visibility (e.g., speaking at events), and help build relationships across the firm—all with the end goal of increasing their billable hours. Whether this solution solves the retention problem over the long term remains to be seen; the firm has only just implemented the program and is now waiting on results. However, early findings (leading measures) seem promising!

In addition to helping explain quantitative data and identify possible solutions, as it did in the previous example, qualitative data is also good for pure discovery. A lot of the time when you're gathering **DEI** data, you won't know what you're looking for until you find it. That's a particular strength of qualitative data over quantitative data: with qualitative data, you don't need to know exactly what you want to measure from the outset. Instead, you can iterate as you collect more data and hone in on patterns that emerge.

But that pattern finding and iteration comes with data analysis. Before we get into analysis, we need to employ some solid methods for collecting qualitative data.

Executive Interviews

When building a DEI program from the ground up—specifically a *data-based* DEI program—one-on-one executive interviews are one of the first things you need to do. Why? Part of it has to do with the C-suite buy-in we discussed in Chapter 3. Interviewing these leaders will help you get a sense of their level of investment and, hopefully, gain increased commitment to DEI as time goes on. This is a fairly subjective data point, but it's important. You won't be able to move forward with an effective DEI program if you're dealing with executives who refuse to champion the initiative and take responsibility for its success. If they're not on board, you need to go back to Chapter 3 and double down on that ground-level work.

Assuming the executives have bought in, the other purpose of these interviews is to get a high-level view of what's currently going on in the organization as well as any historical context that may be getting in the way of DEI progress. What is the culture like? What are its values? What are the strategic initiatives that are being pursued or will be pursued in the near future? What direction is the organization headed toward from **diversity**, **equity**, and **inclusion** standpoints? Who is its target customer base, and is that changing? All of this information forms a baseline that you can then compare to the data you glean from surveys and focus groups to identify whether employees and leadership are in alignment or whether there are any disconnects.

Here are some example questions we ask when conducting executive interviews:

What is your organization's history with DEI?

What long-term impact do you hope to see as a result of your organization's DEI efforts?

What challenges or barriers do you see getting in the way?

How will you hold yourself accountable to being a DEI champion?

The answers you get will not only serve as the foundation for building a more data-driven DEI strategy but will also help ensure that that strategy is later stewarded by the executives who provided this data in the first place.

Open-Ended Survey Questions

In the previous chapter, we discussed surveys at length as a tool for collecting quantitative data. However, there is one type of survey question that can be used to collect qualitative data: the open-ended survey question.

Open-ended survey questions are a great way to collect a large amount of qualitative data in a short amount of time. Focus groups and executive interviews are limited to a few people, whereas open-ended questions go to all survey participants. This means that in a whole-workforce survey, every single person in the organization can conceivably contribute their thoughts. It's also a great way to more immediately understand the "why" behind participants' quantitative responses, where you can leave space for them to elaborate.

A few open-ended items we like are as follows:

What is your organization doing well in terms of advancing DEI?

What can your organization be doing better to advance DEI?

What else would you like to share about DEI at your organization?

Finally, by giving survey participants the option to include open-ended data, you are giving them a voice when it comes to DEI at their organization—an important aspect of fostering an inclusive workplace culture.

Focus Groups

Arguably the most important place you will be asking open-ended questions—albeit orally rather than in writing—is in focus groups.

Focus groups are organized discussions with a select group of individuals meant to gain information about their views and experiences with a certain topic. Unlike in a group interview, where the researcher asks each person in the group to respond to a question in turn, participants in focus groups are encouraged to talk with one another; they can ask questions, exchange anecdotes, comment on what others have said, and otherwise interact in organic ways that arise from open-ended, facilitated, small-group conversations. This is the value of focus groups: they can yield data that an interviewer would never have thought to look for but that is no less relevant and valuable.

The impetus for a focus group is an issue or gap that you uncover through your quantitative data that you're unsure of how to address. DEI practitioner Lindsay Ciancetta shared how this might work:

> *Our quantitative data is important—it's our flashlight. It shows us where, within this world of our organization, we should focus. But it only shows us where to look. It doesn't give us the action that needs to be taken. That's where you need to get into the qualitative data.*

Thus, focus groups offer a way to determine what is causing the gap you discover and possibly also some guidance on the best way to close it. "Focus groups really are my first recommendation is if you want to dig in and understand," said Ciancetta.

When it comes to who should be in a focus group, it's most advantageous to hear from groups of individuals who have less positive DEI data compared to the overall average. For example, one of our clients saw significantly lower **belonging** scores for both Black and LGBTQ+ employees compared to the average scores across the entire workforce. We therefore held identity-specific focus groups with six to eight volunteers (our recommended focus group size to ensure that all voices were heard) who identified with these communities, respectively. We showed the participants the gaps in the survey data and asked them to explain why they thought the numbers played out the way they had. We also asked for concrete recommendations on how to close those gaps. From their responses, we discovered two key areas that the organization needed to improve: (1) they needed more **BIPOC** individuals in senior leader roles, and (2) they needed more education around the importance of inclusive language, especially when it comes to LGBTQ+ terminology.

Recruiting Focus Group Participants

In some cases, it's possible to gather focus group volunteers by including a question at the end of the initial survey, asking whether the respondent would be willing to participate in a follow-up focus group. That way, we're able to draw from a pool of employees who have already expressed willingness to share more about their perceptions of DEI at their organization. (This method requires a **confidential**—not **anonymous**—survey methodology, though.) However, an ideal place to recruit focus group participants is from **employee resource groups** (ERGs).

An ERG, also referred to as a "business resource group" or "affinity group," is an employee-identity or experience-based group that builds community, provides support to its members, and contributes to personal and professional development of its members in the work environment. Organizations, especially large ones, often support the formation of ERGs in order to give underrepresented groups a forum where their voices can be heard and a platform to better self-advocate for their unique needs and concerns. We'll discuss ERGs more in Chapter 13. But for now, if the gaps you're seeing affect groups who already have an ERG, that's an excellent place to recruit focus group participants. The reason is that these groups have already built a subculture of trust that is essential for the sorts of candid conversations necessary to yield meaningful insights.

If your organization doesn't have an ERG from which to recruit the right focus group participants, then you'll need to find a champion: someone who shares the identity you are seeking for the focus group and who is trusted as a leader, whether they're formally recognized as such or not. This is the person you want to tap and ask to assist in outreach to possible focus group participants. "The fact is, if you don't have a recognized ERG in your organization, you have an underground ERG in your organization," said Ciancetta. "It already exists; you just don't know about it. So it's a matter of tapping into that somehow. You need to find the leader of it." With this person in the driver's seat, you can recruit participants through **snowball sampling**: getting existing participants to invite a few people, who then invite a few more people, and so on until you have the number of participants you need.

Conducting Focus Groups

Once you have your focus group of six to eight participants, it's time to start asking them open-ended discussion questions. The questions should be driven by the quantitative data results that you are seeking to explain. For example, the results of one company's **engagement** survey might show lower scores for Asian employees compared to other demographic groups on items measuring perceived manager support and perceived promotion fairness. Additionally, the retention data pulled from human resource information system (HRIS) shows that Asian employees are leaving the company at a higher rate than other groups. Based on that information, you'll know that you want a focus group of Asian employees, and you can craft open-ended questions that focus on those three areas: manager support, opportunities for advancement, and retention. Here are some example questions you could ask:

What could your manager do to make you feel supported?

What would make employees feel there are not equal opportunities at your organization?

Do you have any examples of someone leaving that shared your identity that you really wish had stayed? Why did they leave? Are there things the company could be doing better to keep top performers?

Finally, there's the matter of who is conducting these focus groups. Based on our own experience and that of our clients, we highly recommend bringing in an external party. This not only helps to ensure confidentiality of who participated and their responses, but it also helps participants *trust* that confidentiality, leading to more open and honest responses.

Of course, we recognize that not every organization has the resources to bring in a trained facilitator. You should only consider conducting a focus group yourself if you are skilled at quickly building trust by making others feel safe and comfortable. In this case, be sure to align yourself with the champion we mentioned earlier, who can vouch for you. Lean on them to help engender trust with focus group members, especially if you do not identify with the identity of the group you are interviewing.

Whenever possible, we recommend the facilitator share the identity of the targeted focus group (e.g., have a woman facilitator for a women's focus group, a Black facilitator for a Black focus group, and so on). When matching the facilitator's identity to that of the focus group participants isn't possible, make sure to overtly call out what your being in the room does to the conversation. Your awareness of how you are affecting the space is critical.

A few more pointers for if you will be moderating a focus group:[14]

- You are there to listen. Be careful not to lead the participants in a certain direction through your words, actions, or body language.

- Set expectations for participants regarding the length of the discussion and its purpose.

- Ensure that participants know their participation is confidential and valued. Request their honest responses.

- It is okay for people to disagree! It is important for you to capture all perspectives. Be sure to note when certain answers/topics are especially divisive.

- Take thorough notes. Record the session if possible, in order to reference exact quotes later on. Be sure to maintain high standards of confidentiality and data security to protect participants and respect their right to anonymity.

- Be sure to ask clarifying questions to make sure you are capturing the true essence of their experience by not making any assumptions.

---

14 Before getting started, think through the why, who, and how you'll collect focus group data in Worksheet #7 of our Inclusalytics Workbook, available at www.inclusalytics.com/workbook

- Sometimes, with a quiet group, you may need to ask probing or follow-up questions to coax out more details.

- You may also have a group where someone talks too much. In those scenarios, politely thank them for their contribution, and then ask if anyone else would like to add to what has been said. Emphasize the importance of *all* voices being heard.

Ad Hoc Reporting

In our discussion of quantitative data, we brought up integrative chatbots and other tech tools that can be used to collect data in a more ongoing way. Much of this data is often quantitative in nature (á la **pulse surveys**), but there are ways to use these tools to collect qualitative data as well. For instance, a simple feedback form can be used to allow employees to proactively (and anonymously, if desired) report certain behaviors related to DEI. This could be set up quantitatively, with predefined behaviors to choose from, but it could also be an open-response field, which could yield rich qualitative data.

In many cases where this reporting feature has been set up, it is intended for reporting negative behaviors, such as moments of **bias** or **discrimination**. However, it's important to also enable—and, in fact, encourage—the reporting of *positive* behaviors. Inclusive behaviors like "This person invited me to a networking event" or "This person is the only one who has taken the time to correctly pronounce my name" are valuable and important to record. You don't want to just search for deficiencies within your organization, but also for strengths upon which you can capitalize. If, for instance, certain inclusive behaviors are yielding higher belongingness outcomes than others, you'll want to know what those are so you can put more energy into emphasizing, developing, and holding people accountable to using them!

Show Employees Their Data Matter

At last, we're back to the issues of safety and incentives, which we discussed in Chapter 6. People need to feel safe to be willing to share their views, and they need to feel motivated.

A surefire way to get people *not* to participate in your data collection efforts is to render their efforts futile. In other words, if people spend time and energy giving you feedback on an issue and then never hear about it again, they will feel that their efforts were in vain and will be unlikely to participate in the future. You might have done the best data analysis and identified the world's most effective interventions, but if you don't communicate what was found and what's being done, it will look like a whole lot of nothing. The same goes for if you rush through your data analysis to show your employees, "Look! Here's what we were doing!" Poor data analysis can lead to poor intervention selection, and if employees fail to see any changes, they're not going to be very motivated to fill out yet another survey or waste their time in a focus group.

Conversely, if, after you collect data, you take sufficient time to analyze it and develop an action plan, and *then* you share your findings and your plan (which, not incidentally, are the topics we'll cover next) . . . well, there are no guarantees; but we can say with a fair degree of confidence that when an employee feels like their voice has been heard, it's pretty darn motivating to continue contributing to DEI efforts.

When it comes to doing DEI right, listening is a good start. But action is even better.

CHAPTER 8:
Turn Data into Insights

Now that you have data in hand, it's time to make sense of it. That means analyzing the data and building a narrative that explains your analysis in a way the rest of the organization (especially senior leadership) can understand.

Inclusalytics is ultimately using statistics to answer questions related to **DEI**, especially to figure out how to build a more inclusive workplace culture. This involves (but is not limited to) analyzing the demographic breakdown of the organization, assessing factors that affect personnel selection, measuring how frequently inclusive behaviors are used, or discerning the themes of exit interviews and how they differ by group identification—just to name a few. Essentially, you're conducting analyses that explore how the experiences of identity groups may differ or converge within your organization.

How you analyze your data depends on what questions you are trying to answer. Do you want to know the makeup of your workforce demographics across functions and leader levels? Are you curious if certain identity groups have lower **engagement** or higher turnover compared to the rest of the organization? In the first example you are just exploring descriptive statistics of demographic variables like the average age or percentage of women in your workforce; you are not looking for relationships among variables. This requires a fairly simple analysis of straightforward **diversity** data. Conversely, in the second example, you may be looking to see how identity groups differ in their perceptions of **equity** and if those experiences show any relationship with differences in engagement or turnover. This latter type of analysis is often more useful for creating positive change, but it's also more complex.

If you took our recommendations when you were building and implementing your measurement methods back in Chapter 6, you'll already have someone on deck—whether an external consultant or in-house staff—who is trained in **psychometrics**, statistics, survey design and administration, and data management.

This is the ideal person to run your analyses. Of course, it's not mandatory that your analyst be the same person or team that designed the methods/tools you used to collect your DEI data, but they do need to have some statistical expertise in order to help you draw meaningful conclusions from those data.[15]

Your analyst also needs to be clear about the methods they are using to analyze the data. We'll take a bird's-eye view of what needs to be done when analyzing DEI data in this chapter, but if your analyst cannot explain their methods and the reasoning behind the choices they make, find another analyst! The risks of allowing someone unqualified to run your analyses are substantial, and if you understand the value of DEI work, you'll understand why: not only are there risks to the business (such as the turnover costs we described in Chapter 3; never mind exposure to potential lawsuits), but if you do this work poorly, you'll miss out on key opportunities to improve the livelihoods, work performance, and well-being of employees, especially those from underrepresented groups.

Although data analysis needs to be done *right*, it doesn't need to be complicated. In fact, when analyzing DEI data, simpler is often better. In our industrial-organizational (I-O) psychology training, we learned all sorts of advanced statistical methods, but oftentimes we find them needlessly complex for DEI data analysis. As fellow I-O/DEI expert Lindsay Ciancetta told us: "The best statistic is the one that answers the question you're asking." Sometimes, that can be doing something as simple as visualizing data with a bar chart or a Venn diagram. Any analysis that leads to useful DEI insights is a good analysis!

Cleaning Your Data

The first step in data analysis is to "clean your data." This means making sure you have all variables in one place, clear understanding of what each row, column, and value means, getting rid of duplicate entries (e.g., if the same person submitted a survey twice), and deciding how to handle missing data.

Missing data is a big issue in **quantitative data** analysis, specifically when analyzing surveys. It happens when an employee—we'll call him "Bill"—fills out one part of the survey but not the whole thing. There are a few ways to handle this. One is to drop Bill's survey from the results entirely. The downside to this approach is that you'll lose his responses to the first part of the survey, which will decrease your overall sample size, as well as eliminate Bill's voice from the items he *did* answer. Imagine if Bill were caring for an ailing parent. He started

---

15 Not sure who is the best person to analyze DEI data at *your* organization? Then work through the decision tree in Worksheet #8 of our Inclusalytics Workbook, available at www.inclusalytics. com/workbook

the survey, but when he put his phone down to attend to his parent, the link expired. By eliminating his answers, you'll eliminate any unique insights he may have shared as a working male caregiver.

However, if you retain only the questions Bill completed, your overall sample size won't match for the entire survey. For example, if he answered the diversity questions but not the equity or **inclusion** questions, you might have 100 people in your diversity sample but only 99 people in your equity or inclusion sample. Extrapolate this to a several-thousand-person organization where any number of people might skip any number of survey questions, and the issue of missing data and differing sample sizes gets messy.

There are a variety of statistical methods for handling missing data, something every good data analyst should have in their toolbox. The key is to be transparent about what you did to account for missing data and to have a sound reason for choosing that method that you are able to explain and justify. You can also make every item on a survey required, which removes the possibility of missing data. But remember: if the "Bills" in the organization fail to complete the survey, then this "solution" removes their voice entirely!

INCLUSALYTICS CALLOUT

If you make responses mandatory, be sure to include an escape option such as "Choose not to answer" or "Don't know" for people who are uncomfortable responding to an item.

One last thing about missing data before we move on: who does and does not respond to a survey, or even part of a survey, is data itself. This is called a **nonresponse pattern**. Let's say your DEI survey gets an 85 percent response rate. That's a great rate, and certainly worth celebrating! (In the context of an employee survey, anything over 70 percent is very good.) However, if, when you look into who comprised the missing 15 percent, it's 90 percent of all of your Black employees (which you figured out by comparing survey responses to your human resource information system (HRIS) data), that signifies a problem. Why did this group not take the survey? Do they not trust the survey process? Do they think nothing will come of it? Or what if the missing 15 percent is not Black employees, but all middle managers? Do they think the survey is unimportant? Do they feel like they don't have time to take it? These are important issues you'll need to uncover and address before your next DEI survey goes out. This is why DEI work is forever ongoing: your data analysis will inevitably reveal something that you then need to investigate, attempt to fix, measure, and measure again!

Analyzing Quantitative Data

Once your data is "clean," it's time to dig in and figure out what it's saying. This is not a statistics textbook, so we aren't going to get into all of the fancy statistics you can apply. For that, we recommend checking out the following resources:[16]

The Basic Terminologies of Statistics You Should Know
Rupam Choudhary
statanalytica.com/blog/terminologies-of-statistics

- This is a quick interactive primer that will introduce you to basic statistical terminology and concepts.

HR Analytics in R: Common Tasks Achieved with the Power of R
Chester Ismay, Albert Y. Kim, and Hendrik Feddersen
hranalyticslive.netlify.app

- This self-guided (free!) course teaches you how to use R and RStudio—powerful and open-source data software tools—for data analysis and visualization. By presenting examples of real data sets that apply to HR analytics, this resource also helps you learn how to make decisions based off data.

R for Data Science
Hadley Wickham and Garrett Grolemund
r4ds.had.co.nz

- Based on Wickham and Grolemund's 2017 book, *R for Data Science*, this web resource offers a more technical introduction to R with in-depth data manipulation, visualization, and model building.

7 HR Data Sets for People Analytics
Erik van Vulpen
aihr.com/blog/hr-data-sets-people-analytics

- Here you'll find seven online data sets related to people analytics that you can use to practice.

---

16 Note: We do not recommend using these tools without at least some foundational training in statistics and data science. Is there a data analyst within your organization you could bring on to help you with this work? Or an external resource you can hire to build you a scalable process? (See more in the section on dashboards in the following chapter.)

Handbook of Regression Modeling in People Analytics
Keith McNulty
peopleanalytics-regression-book.org

- This resource is a free version of McNulty's 2021 book of the same name. It teaches both R and Python (a multipurpose programming language) with examples focused on people analytics.

Instead, what we are going to do is offer a few key pointers and some examples of what you might look for when you perform Inclusalytics—that is, when you apply statistics to detect patterns and predict relationships between variables using quantitative DEI data.

Statistical Significance and Effect Size

When you start slicing your numerical data by group—and remember that a group identity doesn't always need to be something visible or common, like gender or race; it can include unseen attributes like tenure at the organization, leader level, business unit, geographical location, and so on—there will always be groups that score lower than average on a given measure. Even if everyone scores high relative to the scale (e.g., over a 5 on a 1–10 scale), some groups will always score "less favorably" than the others. That's what an average is, after all: the aggregated range of scores, with some groups being lower and higher than the collective average.

Ideally, you'll want to assess whether the less favorable subgroup scores you find are **statistically significant**. In other words, if you have a large enough sample and a critical p value or a confidence interval that excludes the null hypothesis value (which you can learn more about from those resources we shared), then that group's low score is highly unlikely to be due to chance or random factors, meaning that you need to look into it. (If it's not statistically significant, then you may need to gather more data, or else you can move on to other concerns that *are* statistically significant!) We recommend working with a data analyst to ensure that you run any significant tests correctly.

Besides statistical significance, another way to determine if your finding is meaningful is to measure **effect size**. Effect size is, essentially, the size of a difference between populations (e.g., retention rate between millennial versus boomer populations) or the strength of an association between two variables in the same population (e.g., does giving millennials food at work impact their retention rate?). To answer the question of whether a difference is large or an association is strong, there needs to be some sort of parameter for comparison.

One option is to compare the effect you find to effects other researchers or DEI practitioners have found pertaining to that measurement (e.g., millennial retention) from peer-reviewed journal articles. This is also where industry-benchmarking or even year-over-year internal benchmarking could come in handy.

Adverse Impact

Now let's get into what you might look for amidst all of your number crunching. Companies are legally obligated to look out for something called **adverse impact**, so let's dig into that.

Adverse impact, also called "disparate impact," is the effect of a hiring selection process (hiring, promotions, etc.) that (1) creates a substantially different rate of employment decisions (2) to the disadvantage of members of protected groups. Equal Employment Opportunity (EEO) protected groups include race, color, religion, sex (including pregnancy, sexual orientation, or gender identity), national origin, age (forty or older), and disability and genetic information (including family medical history). Basically, any selection process that hurts the employment opportunities of members of a protected group and thus disproportionately screens them out is unlawfully discriminatory unless that selection process can be shown to be necessary to perform the job.

Take, for instance, testing for written English competence. Such a test would screen out many non-native English speakers such as new immigrants. If the demographic group (e.g., new immigrants) were shown to be selected at less than 80 percent of the rate at which the overrepresented group (native English speakers) was selected, that would be considered adverse impact. Such a test would be unlawful in the case of a cashier job, where writing in English is not necessary to perform that job. However, it would be considered a legal selection criterion for a job that requires writing in English, such as journalism.[17]

(See Figure 9) Here's an example that shows how to calculate whether adverse impact is occurring: Fifty male applicants are chosen from a pool of one hundred qualified male applicants (selection ratio = 50/100 = 50 percent). If twenty-five female applicants are chosen from a pool of one hundred qualified female applicants (selection ratio = 25/100 = 25 percent), then female applicants are hired at 50 percent, or half the rate that male applicants are hired. In this case, adverse impact has occurred because the hiring rate for female applicants is less than 80 percent of the hiring rate for male applicants (i.e., 25/100 is less than 80

---

17 This principle was adopted by the Supreme Court in 1971 in the case of *Griggs v. Duke Power Co.* and was ratified and endorsed by Congress when it passed the U.S. Equal Employment Opportunity Act of 1972.

percent of 50/100). If women had been hired at 80 percent of the rate of male applicants, their selection ratio would have been 40 percent, and 40 out of 100 qualified female applicants would have been hired.

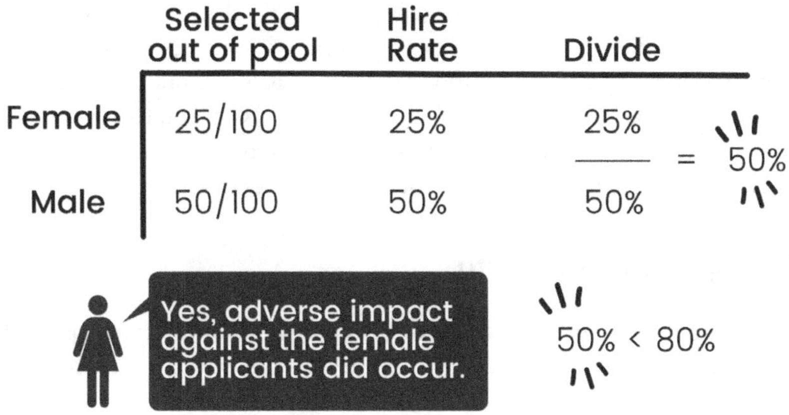

	Selected out of pool	Hire Rate	Divide
Female	25/100	25%	25%
Male	50/100	50%	50%

$$\frac{25\%}{50\%} = 50\%$$

Yes, adverse impact against the female applicants did occur.

50% < 80%

Figure 9

Suffice to say, adverse impact is likely something your organization is already tracking because it is so legally contentious. It provides a good example of the ways Inclusalytics can be useful! And it further reinforces the need for valid measures of DEI, because in the United States, **validity** evidence is required for defending selection measures (like that written English test) in case they are found to have adverse impact. Not that fear of being sued should be the primary motivator to conduct valid DEI research—but it can't be overlooked either.

Who Is (and Isn't) Responding

One final note on quantitative data analysis: when dealing with numbers, it's easy to get caught up in big effects that come from correspondingly big sample sizes (i.e., very large populations). "Two thousand people gave this response," or "85 percent of our organization says this," make for eye-catching headlines. But remember: your underrepresented groups will inherently have smaller response counts because they have smaller head counts. (They're underrepresented, after all.)

To avoid missing out on what these smaller groups have to say, we suggest paying more attention to their response *percentage*. For example, if eight Black women say that they don't feel there are equal opportunities in your organization, that may seem low compared to the two hundred white women who said that opportunities are equal. However, if there are only ten Black women in your organization, 80 percent of them are seeing opportunities as inequitable, which is a staggering proportion.

And then there's the issue of who actually provided the data you are working with. Let's say that according to survey results, 85 percent of your veteran employees said they feel respected at your organization. That's fantastic . . . until you realize only 30 percent of veteran employees filled out the survey. Now you can't assume all is well. The silence of the 70 percent paints a far different picture—one that's your responsibility to go back and investigate in order to understand.

Analyzing Qualitative Data

When it comes to **qualitative data** (e.g., **focus group** or interview data), there are a number of analysis methods you can use. The one we've found most useful is **thematic analysis**.

Thematic analysis involves looking at qualitative responses, like answers to open-ended questions on a survey or interview transcripts, and looking for themes across them. This is called "coding." Johnny Saldaña's (2016) book *The Coding Manual for Qualitative Researchers* is a great resource for more information on coding and exploring themes in your DEI data. Broadly, the process can look something like this: First, start by "marinating in the data." This involves reading and rereading the data and considering emerging findings. Then, go through all the qualitative responses and write down themes you see. These themes should be broad—"communication," for instance. At this point, the answers contributing to your theme don't need to match in terms of sentiment. One person might describe communication within the organization in a negative way, and one person might describe it in a positive way; both answers would contribute to "communication" as the theme you are finding. You could then split the "communication" theme into subthemes like "effective communication" and "poor communication."

Now, when we say "you" can do these things, we actually mean two or three "yous" who have been trained in coding data. In academia, we call these people "coders." Each coder comes up with themes independently, and then all come together to compare findings. What themes did you find in common? What themes differed? Many times, this multiple-coder practice can reveal **bias**—an inclination or predisposition for or against something—on the part of individual coders. Bias is inevitable because we are all humans who bring our own unique experiences to bear when we do anything, even our attempts to objectively code data. For example, if you're a working parent, you're going to be more likely to notice answers related to parental leave. That's not necessarily a bad thing! But it is important to verify whether that theme is as salient as you believe it to be. This is the reason for having multiple coders comparing results: it helps you come as close as possible to seeing what's "really there" in the data.

The second step in thematic analysis involves digging deeper into each agreed-upon theme to see which respondents feel a certain way about that theme and how strongly they feel. For example, maybe the communication theme came up only for upper management and for entry-level workers. Upper management thinks communication is fine; they write answers like, "We talk to our employees regularly about expectations and are transparent about why we are doing DEI work." Meanwhile, entry-level workers think communication is terrible; they write answers like, "Communication from management is very poor." This discrepancy would warrant further exploration, perhaps via focus groups.

Likewise, just because a theme doesn't show up frequently doesn't mean that it's not important. If 98 percent of survey respondents leave the open-ended question about communication blank, but the 2 percent who fill it in are saying "Communication from management is very poor," then something's still happening there that may be worth investigating—especially if those comments are coming from individuals that identify as members of underrepresented/historically disadvantaged groups.

Finally, there's one more way to go about this process of analysis. Thanks to advancements in machine learning, it is now possible to use AI to perform thematic analysis—called "topic modeling" when performed by statistical software—without any human intervention (thereby potentially reducing human bias!). Data analysis programs like R, NVivo, and Atlas.ti pull out words based on frequency, show how closely those words relate, and group them by topic, often using visual displays.[18] You can run these programs alone, or you can use them to cross-check against human coding of qualitative data. Moreover, without the need to rely on human time and energy to code, you can use machine learning to analyze really large data sets more efficiently! Be aware, however, that these tools are not for data novices, and a skilled analyst or I-O psychologist will still need to interpret the results.

---

18 For more information, see the article, "A Review of Best Practice Recommendations for Text Analysis in R (and a User-Friendly App)" published in *Journal of Business and Psychology* (Banks et al. 2018).

Below is an example of what the output from a thematic analysis could look like. (See Figure 10) Imagine you were analyzing open-ended comments from a recent DEI survey. After you did your thematic analysis you wanted to succinctly and intuitively share your findings, so you created the below data visualization. Each ring represents a main theme, whereas each solid circle represents a subtheme. The size of each circle also represents how often that theme came up. Take the "inclusive leadership" theme, for example. The two subthemes were (1) seeking resources to lead more inclusively, and (2) needing more understanding on why inclusive leadership is important. More people had comments related to subtheme #1, which is why that circle is bigger than subtheme #2. We also recommend including a few actual comments from the survey—but only if what was said does not risk identifying who said it.

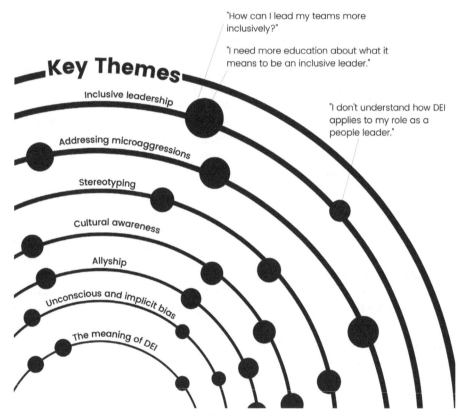

Figure 10

Looking at Intersectionality

In our discussions of analyzing quantitative and qualitative data, we talked a lot about looking at phenomena "by group." We then gave examples using single-attribute groups like parental status, gender, and employment level. However, this is only a first step when performing Inclusalytics. Yes, you need to break apart data by group, but you need to create groupings based not just on a single identity but rather *combinations* of identities. You need to look at your data through an *intersectional* lens.

To refresh your memory, **intersectionality** is the way social categorizations such as race, class, and gender overlap to create interdependent systems of **discrimination** or disadvantage. The lesson here is that people are more than one aspect of their identity: they can be homosexual Asian moms, Latino millennial managers, white single veterans, or any number of other combinations. Because there are so many possible combinations, how you group them when you analyze your data matters, and the more ways you can slice the data, the better. It's fine to split up data by race—that's a start. But it's *just* a start. You're likely going to get more meaning, and better outcomes, if you can layer on additional attributes to figure out exactly who is being left out, undervalued, or otherwise neglected.

One of our clients described the importance of investigating intersectionality when their company conducted its first DEI survey. When analyzing the questions measuring **belonging**, they found that overall, their Black population scored the lowest of all racial groups. However, when they stratified that racial (Black) group by other features, they uncovered something surprising: Black managers scored just as high on belonging as anyone else at the company. Those managers clearly felt like they belonged. Meanwhile, Black individual contributors were scoring so low that they had tanked the score of the whole racial group. So it wasn't *all* Black employees who didn't feel like they belonged, it was Black individual contributors—a fact that wasn't apparent until the client looked at intersectionality within the data.

Understanding the Story

The next question our client needed to ask was why Black individual contributors were feeling left out. This is when qualitative data is at its best: only by asking those contributors about their experiences could the company hope to understand what was hurting their sense of belonging.

"My key is don't just look at the data—make sure you understand the story," said Cheryl Kleppner, a talent acquisition expert who has led DEI efforts at multiple technology and manufacturing companies. She emphasized that the story underlying DEI trends can be affected by any number of business practices.

For instance, if you see upticks in overall diversity around certain times of the year, that might be due to specific hiring practices like university recruiting cycles. Crunching the tenure-related diversity data would tell you that your most recent applicant pools and new hires have more diverse **representation** than in the past. But only by talking to those hires or doing other qualitative research will you understand why this is taking place (e.g., successful recruiting from more diverse universities) and whether or not it might be problematic. If your diversity metrics are improving only because of university recruits, then it's only your entry-level hires who are getting more diverse. If these hires are dissatisfied and don't stick around, then your upper ranks will never diversify, and the cycle can become a self-fulfilling prophecy: new recruits won't see themselves in the upper-level positions at your organization, so they'll leave before they get to those ranks, only to be replaced by new recruits who won't see themselves in upper-level positions. . . . The only way to break this cycle is to understand the story behind it.

Identifying Gaps and Strengths

As we touched on in Chapter 4, it's important to not only identify gaps in your DEI data, but also to look at where the organization is doing well. "When you look at where you're doing well it allows you to also dig into what's being done in those locations or those approaches that you can mirror in other places," said Kleppner. That's what one of her employers did: they looked at data from their ten largest US locations where their workforce was based and drilled down to see where there was good equity across populations. Specifically, they wanted to see if there were particular hiring teams that were doing a good job attracting and retaining diverse talent. By doing this, they could identify and replicate best practices across the business.

Once they identified where their best results were coming from, the company dug deeper into qualitative research, conducting interviews with the HR staff leading those teams' hiring efforts. Among those hiring teams with the best DEI metrics, here were the commonalities they found:

- The hiring team explicitly focused on diverse outreach
- The team had undergone DEI training
- The panel conducting the interviews was itself diverse
- Leadership and management overseeing the team understood the business case for DEI

By identifying these attributes, Kleppner and her DEI team could then go back and expand these best practices across the organization. They provided all hiring teams with DEI training, helped them ensure that their interview panels were diverse, and guided them through building business cases for DEI that the teams could present to various leadership groups responsible for the employee lifecycle.

Measuring ROI

In addition to identifying where your organization is falling short or excelling in DEI, you're going to want to conduct analyses that answer the age-old business question: Are you seeing return on investment? As we touched on in Chapter 3, DEI leaders are often asked to demonstrate ROI before they'll be granted a DEI budget. Whether or not that was you, you'll most certainly be asked about ROI after interventions are put in place. Therefore, you want to build in **impact measures** from the outset. What is the measurable impact you want to see as the result of a specific DEI intervention? What data will you collect to assess that impact? And how can you tie that impact to the business's bottom line?

Answering this question is not always easy because, as you already know, not everything can be quantified or assigned a dollar amount. "Productivity" and "engagement" can be particularly elusive when it comes to tying them directly back to monetary figures. Still, this is an exercise that needs to be done, so let's walk through an example.

The cost of your DEI program is $25,000/year. During the three-year period after the launch of this program, you see a decrease in turnover resulting in the need to hire ten fewer employees compared to three years ago. The average cost to onboard a new employee is $4,000, so your net savings over three years—without even considering the cost to *hire* new employees, which we covered in Chapter 3—is $40,000. Your ROI calculation is the savings divided by the costs:

$40,000 / ($25,000 x 3) = 53% ROI

Now, it's important not to confuse correlation with causation. The decrease in turnover is *correlated with* (i.e., has a relationship with), not necessarily *caused by*, the launch of your DEI program. Your new DEI program might be the cause, but until you have valid, reliable measures in place demonstrating that your company's DEI work is causing people to have higher engagement and belonging scores and thereby stay at the company longer, you cannot know for sure whether one thing is causing the other. (Remember our soapbox in Chapter 6 about creating valid and reliable measurement tools? This is why!)

Now, let's say that you measured turnover intentions in your annual DEI survey in the years after launching your DEI program. That is one way you might be able to tie the DEI program to causation: people might explicitly tell you in the survey that they stayed, in part, due to the DEI program. Another way is to run regression analyses. Your data analyst colleagues or consultants will be familiar with these, but they're essentially a statistical method of figuring out which of a bunch of possible variables correlates most closely with an outcome.

In our example, the outcome we're trying to understand—or, in more scientific terms, the **dependent variable**—is employee retention. Any number of things might cause employees to stay at an organization: their age, the size of their bonus, the job market, the cost of buying a home . . . you name it. When running a linear regression analysis, you want to collect data on as many of the factors you suspect are influencing your dependent variable, plot that data on a chart, and see how closely you can fit a line to the data. The better the fit, the tighter the correlation.[19] (Again, you can't claim causation here, but you'll have sounder mathematics behind the relationship between your DEI program and employee retention.) There are some other factors to consider when conducting regression analyses such as control variables and nonlinear data patterns...which you can learn more about in the stats resources we provided.

Are You Making Progress?

You can ask any number of questions as you analyze your DEI data, but the final and arguably most important question you'll want to answer is, "Are we making progress toward our DEI goals?" This is the elusive "moving the needle" claim that so many DEI leaders strive to achieve. When you attempt to answer this question, there are several possible trends you'll find. The first is the simplest: there is no change. This could indicate a number of things. Maybe you haven't given your interventions enough time to work.[20] Maybe you chose ineffective interventions. Maybe your analyses are flawed. Or maybe you're trying to solve the wrong problem. This is a case where you'll need to go back and review everything from your methods of collecting data, to the data itself, to who analyzed the data and how, to what interventions you chose, and who participated in them. This is a frustrating position to be in, but take heart—every DEI practitioner we spoke to referenced the need for patience and perseverance. "This is a marathon, not a sprint," said Michelle Wimes, chief equity and inclusion officer at Children's Mercy Hospital in Kansas City, Missouri. "It's so easy to get discouraged; it's so easy to get overwhelmed. But I think it's really important to keep in mind, Rome wasn't built in a day."

---

19 For the sake of brevity, we're seriously oversimplifying this process. For a more thorough yet accessible explanation, check out the *Harvard Business Review* article, "A Refresher on Regression Analysis."

20 We take the same stance as Cascio and Aguinis (2011) and recommend waiting a minimum of three months after a DEI behavior change intervention before assessing whether there is an increase in these behaviors back on the job. It's also important to recognize that for these behaviors to take root as part of an organization's *culture* can take years (Kotter 1995).

The second trend you might see is also straightforward: gaps that you identified where the underrepresented group scores were lower than the overrepresented group are closing. "It seems so simple, but that's it," said Ciancetta. "We're just looking to close the gap. And that means we are changing the experience and the culture for people."

The change can be dramatic, but it doesn't need to be. Here's an example from one of our clients: In 2019, 3 percent of this organization's managers were **BIPOC**, and 3 percent of its new management-level hires were BIPOC. The organization wanted to improve diversity in its managerial ranks in order to better match the racial makeup of the business as a whole, but they knew they couldn't make double-digit changes overnight, or even within a year—the company wasn't growing (and/or losing non-BIPOC managers) fast enough for that. However, they *could* look at the proportion of new hires coming in and try to increase that ratio.

In 2020, the organization implemented a rule to make sure BIPOC candidates were being added to the hiring pipeline at the interview stage. That year, their percentage of new BIPOC managerial hires increased from 3 percent to 10 percent. By 2021, the organization's overall ratio of BIPOC managers increased from 3 percent to 3.5 percent. This might not look like a lot, but it's a ratio that's trending in the right direction, and that, if it continues over time, will show increasingly significant impact.

Seeing diversity gaps close is one thing, but sometimes, one group may increase while another decreases. This isn't necessarily a bad thing. As our client saw, by increasing BIPOC hires from 3 to 10 percent, non-BIPOC hires had to correspondingly decrease from 97 to 90 percent. (A ratio must always add up to 100!) Especially if you're benchmarking against industry standards or trying to better reflect the pool of potential applicants or local populations, these ratios will likely *need* to change to get to a place of representation.

However, you don't want to see this "one group increases while the other decreases" trend in areas like inclusion or belonging, where there is no "100 percent" total to meet. Remember, workplace inclusion is not a zero-sum game. If the overrepresented group's scores on these measures are decreasing as an underrepresented group's scores increase, this is an indicator that the approach you're taking with your DEI initiatives is alienating your overrepresented group. Ciancetta said she would take this very seriously,

Because it also means you are disenfranchising your change champions, your allies, which is critical for meaningfully shifting culture towards greater inclusion. You don't want that to be happening, because you are creating the perception of the zero-sum game and making your overrepresented-group employees feel like they may not have as much of a place in the organization.

In other words, if your DEI initiatives are improving the underrepresented group's experience at the expense of the overrepresented group, they're going to create new DEI issues down the line—namely **backlash**, or reactance to DEI efforts by overrepresented group members. Backlash has three primary origins: perceived or actual restriction of independence or autonomy, preference for the status quo, and beliefs that gender, racial, and other social equalities have been reached and persistent inequalities are therefore either not present or are merely individual and not structural problems. No matter the origin, backlash will undermine your DEI efforts, so stay vigilant.

INCLUSALYTICS CALLOUT

Be sure to include and monitor overrepresented group members' voices in your DEI efforts to ensure that you understand their perceptions of DEI to counteract any feelings of exclusion or backlash. Pull them in as allies and show them how DEI benefits everyone—not just those from historically disadvantaged groups.

An even worse situation is where the overrepresented group's scores decrease while the underrepresented group's scores stay the same. This will still look like a "gap closing," but now your DEI efforts aren't working for anyone and are only doing harm!

Finally, there's one more possibility: overall scores (e.g., engagement) are going up for the underrepresented group, but the gap isn't necessarily closing because the overrepresented group's scores are *also* going up. This is a case of "rising tides lift all boats," which in some ways is a good outcome. If you're improving the experience of your least represented group, you'll oftentimes improve the experience for everyone.

In our engagement example, let's say low scores are traced back to managers doing a poor job connecting with BIPOC employees. If you teach managers better skills for connecting with their BIPOC employees, they're naturally going to use some of those skills to better connect with *all* of their employees. Ergo, everyone's engagement score rises! However, if overall scores are going up but the gap between your BIPOC employees' engagement scores and your white employees' engagement scores persists, then you haven't actually solved the DEI-specific problem. Your managers might have learned better general management skills, but they're still not connecting on the same level with BIPOC and white employees.

As you can see, the findings you uncover during data analysis are not always going to be positive. In fact, those **privileged** to see initial findings might be ashamed or even horrified by what they find. But the answer is not to gloss over or bury these findings. The people who are experiencing exclusion and disenfranchisement know what's happening whether you broadcast it or not. And while many organizations will still be very careful with what DEI data they release broadly, we have found transparency to be the best policy for organizations that are genuinely working toward meaningful change. That's why this next chapter is so important. Data collection and analysis all go on behind closed doors; DEI reports are how you share your findings with the world.

CHAPTER NINE:
Share Insights to Inspire Action

To make sure the insights you gained from your analysis lead to real changes, you need to share your findings in a compelling way to various audiences. Until others can see and understand what you've discovered, the data are essentially useless.

The two most common ways to display and make sense of your analyzed data are an interactive dashboard or a **static report**. We'll cover dashboards first. Dashboards are "easier" in that once you build the dashboard (which is the hard, resource-intensive part), you can hit "refresh" and the data are automatically updated. This is the dashboard's advantage: it's dynamic and sustainable. It is preprogrammed and it outputs easy-to-digest visuals that help answer your **DEI** questions and monitor your objectives with relevant, timely data. Yet because they are so comprehensive and because they autopopulate (rather than being curated), dashboards are also typically only made accessible internally on a need-to-know basis. Other outward-facing reports might be generated from the data a dashboard provides, but it's usually only DEI leaders, the HR/people analytics team, or senior-level executives who access the dashboard itself.

The other type of report we'll cover is what we'll call the "static" report. These reports are the ones that get distributed to employees, provided to shareholders, presented to boards, and posted on the organization's website. They're most often presented as a PDF report or as a slide deck. We recommend communicating DEI objectives and progress regularly throughout the year (more on that later); but at a bare minimum, an annual report is a must. This report is where you'll share your strategy, discoveries, progress, and future intentions, as well as any impact you're having externally on your industry, community, etc. It can be a heavy lift—especially since you'll be communicating with folks who aren't necessarily familiar with DEI vocabulary, some of whom won't read anything beyond the executive summary, while others will scrutinize even the most minor footnote—but if you're going to do DEI right, communication to *all* stakeholders is a key component. Static reports are a great tool to share your commitment to and progress toward building a more diverse, equitable, and inclusive organization with the world.

DEI Dashboards

Because static reports are most easily generated *from* dashboards, we're going to start this discussion with dashboards. A **DEI dashboard** is a visual summary of the DEI, HR, and other data you have collected (or are collecting) and analyzed. Its purpose is to show, at a fairly high level—and with the ability to narrow down—where your organization is in relation to where you'd like to be when it comes to DEI goals and outcomes. (See Figure 11)

Think of the dashboard on your car: it doesn't tell you the nitty gritty calculations it's making, like electrical current generated by gear movement or the resistance level of the "float" in your gas tank. Instead, it shows you a single miles-per-hour number and a simple fuel gauge graphic so that, at a glance, you can see if you're over the speed limit and whether or not you need to swing by a gas station. Similarly, a DEI dashboard displays the output you need to make high-level, data-driven decisions about DEI in your organization. Using graphs, charts, and infographic-type visuals, a dashboard makes ongoing data consolidation and analysis quicker, easier, and more digestible, resulting in more timely and actionable insights.

We included the first page of an anonymized dashboard we've built for clients below. As you can see, the dashboard is visibly labeled at the top, the data collection method is identified, and all of the data are clearly labeled for easy interpretation. In this example, the focus is around the demographic breakdown of an organization, but dashboards can also include more complex analyses of other variables (e.g., feelings of belongingness) and even show year-over-year differences.

The more data you collect, the more this sort of automation makes sense. Between human resource information system (HRIS) data (e.g., demographics, hiring rates, promotion differences between groups), employee data (e.g., **pulse surveys**, **engagement** surveys, performance evaluations), and internal app data (e.g., emails, calendar invites), there could be a *lot* of data flowing into your DEI dashboard at any given time. Relying on human processing in such a situation would be quite inefficient—by the time you manage to transform the data into something usable, it will be outdated, and in the interim, the problem may have become much bigger!

Creating a dashboard can be a time- and resource-intensive process, but it's a long-term investment that pays dividends. Using a dashboard will give you a clear, up-to-date display of the output of all the number crunching that goes on "under the hood," allowing you to better drive your DEI strategy in real time.

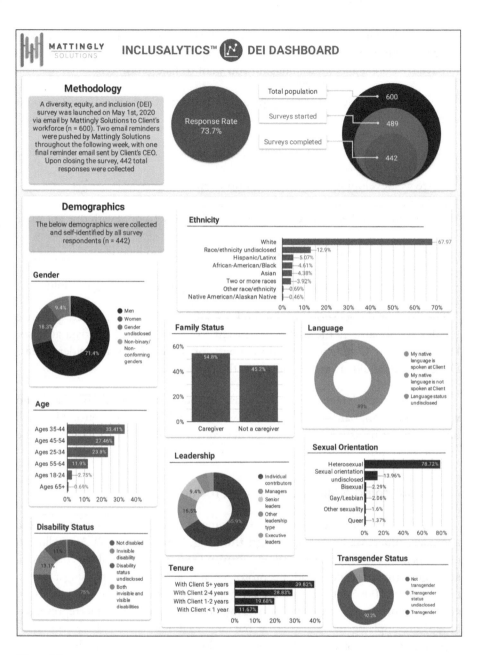

Figure 11

Initial Questions

If you're looking to build a brand-new DEI dashboard, you'll want to start with the end in mind. What are you trying to accomplish? What questions do you want to have answered, and what things do you want to take action on?

Here are examples of some specific questions your organization might want to answer:

How many people from underrepresented groups are applying to open roles?

Are we developing and providing opportunities equitably?

Are leaders and employees using more inclusive behaviors with one another?

Are people feeling more valued, respected, seen, and heard?

Is the rate of underrepresented employees voluntarily quitting declining?

The other early questions you should ask are: Who is the intended audience for this dashboard? Is the dashboard meant to be a tool for DEI data analysts, HR leaders, the C-suite and board members, or some other stakeholder group? Dashboards should always be built with the end user in mind.

These two considerations—the information you are trying to uncover and who will use the dashboard—will impact how you build your dashboard. They will dictate what it measures, what it looks like, and most importantly, how it will be used to drive DEI decisions.

Brainstorming a Minimum Viable Product

To build your DEI dashboard, we recommend taking a hands-on user-centric approach, otherwise known as **design thinking**.[21] (See Figure 12) According to user experience (UX) experts, Nielsen Norman Group, design thinking consists of six stages: empathize, define, ideate, prototype, test, and implement. Using a few of our examples above, let's say you are designing your dashboard for HR end users, and you want to answer the question "How many people from underrepresented groups are applying to open roles at our organization?" Here is how you could apply the six stages of design thinking to develop your DEI dashboard:

---

21 Learn more about Nielsen Norman's Design Thinking Framework at https://www.nngroup. com/articles/design-thinking/

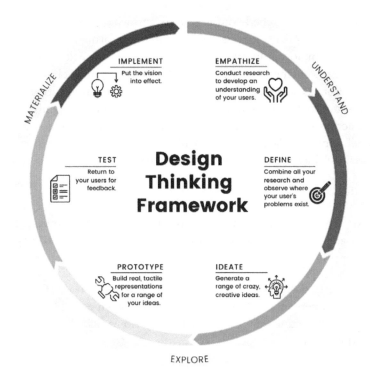

Figure 12

(1) Empathize

To empathize, you must get to know your end user, in this case, your HR employees. Have one-on-one meetings with different HR team members to learn what is going well with their existing DEI data review process and where there is room for improvement. How are they currently recruiting potential employees? What groups are underrepresented in the organization, especially compared to local geographic or broader industry-wide **representation** data? How is this information currently being tracked and shared? What data do they currently wish they had easy access to? How tech- and stat-savvy are they? What are their pain points when it comes to using DEI data?

(2) Define

Now that you've researched your end users and what their needs are, you can begin to define potential solutions. Take all of the information you've obtained from your HR employee interviews and begin to organize it into themes and solutions to those themes. For example, HR needs a high-level view as to how the organization as a whole is attracting (or not attracting) applicants from underrepresented groups to test new recruitment strategies and assess how they work across the entire organization. You'll therefore need to find a way to combine all applicant data into the dashboard design. But what possible data sources are available? That's where the next step comes in.

(3) Ideate

The next step is to brainstorm everything you might want to measure or track in order to answer your question, "How many people from underrepresented groups are applying to open roles?"

We recommend doing this as a live, collaborative workshop. If you conduct the workshop in person, use Post-it notes to write down each idea. If you meet virtually, use a program that has virtual sticky notes, like Miro or Microsoft Whiteboard in Teams.

Some ideas that come up during this ideation phase may include:

- How many applicants are applying from different identities, including a way to look at this data intersectionally
- Where your applicants are coming from, and analyzing origins by identity
- What roles/departments different applicants are applying for by identity
- Diversity of your recruiters

When you've exhausted your imagination, group like ideas with like, and, using those categories, prioritize must-haves over nice-to-haves. This will help you narrow down the most important features to include when you begin the prototyping process.

(4) Prototype

To make sure the final dashboard sufficiently answers your question and meets your HR users' needs, we recommend going into the dashboard-building process with the intention to work through *iterations* of your dashboard. This reduces the pressure to "get everything right" the first time, and it enables you to get started much faster than if you try to build everything you anticipate you might need all at once.

If you can take this iterative approach, you'll start with the minimum viable product (MVP): What are the three to five most essential things you need to measure and track over time? And do you have access to the data you need to measure and track those things? (As we discussed in Chapter 4, access to data often dictates what is or isn't possible!) Using this iterative approach allows you to establish a "build, measure, learn" feedback loop, a concept popularized by Eric Ries in his Lean Startup model. The idea is to build the MVP in the prototype phase, put it in front of a few of your end users for initial reactions (which intersects with the "test" phase of design thinking), learn from the feedback data how to improve upon the prototype (the "implement" phase of design thinking), and continue the loop by revising those initial features or adding new ones. Like we said—iterate!

(5) Test

Now it's time to test out that MVP with all of your end users, which, in this scenario, are your HR employees. Have them use the MVP and observe how intuitive it is to use. Are the features easy to interpret? Are the HR employees able to easily track how many applicants are from underrepresented groups? This is when you enter the *measure* part of Ries's feedback loop. From these data collected, you can *learn* and adjust as needed. Repeat this process until you land on the most user-friendly version of the MVP.

(6) Implement

Once you've reviewed user feedback to decide what your dashboard should include, it's time to engage in stage six of design thinking: implementation. If your organization has a data analysis team, this is when you'll partner with them; if not, it's time to bring in an external data scientist, ideally someone who specializes in building dashboards. Together, you'll need to choose a data visualization tool to render your dashboard. Based on the organizations we spoke with, Tableau and Power BI are the most popular (and our preference), but Google Data and ClickView are other options we've seen work well. There are even organizations who build completely custom dashboards from scratch.

With tight deadlines—and budgets!—it may sometimes be tempting to jump right to implementation without doing all the user experiences research we outlined using Nielsen Norman Group's model above. However, taking a design thinking approach will end up saving you time and money in the long run by building the right dashboard the first time for your end users.

Building the Dashboard

Regardless of what program or company you use to build the dashboard, there are several components that you'll want to include along with the data you're tracking. This list from Tony Cooley, a fellow industrial-organizational (I-O) psychologist and **analytics** consultant who has built a number of DEI dashboards for various organizations, is not exhaustive, but it covers the essentials:

1. **Dashboard name**—This one seems obvious, but if we've learned one thing, it's that some of the most obvious steps in the **Inclusalytics** process get skipped! Don't forget to name your dashboard, especially if your organization uses multiple dashboards for different purposes.

2. **Purpose statement**—This doesn't need to be long, but it does need to be specified. Think back to those initial questions we covered. What are you trying to accomplish? What questions are you trying to answer with *this* dashboard? Those priorities go in your purpose statement. By putting them in black and white, you can help prevent scope creep (i.e., expanding the initial agreed-upon parameters of what the dashboard will and will not include) and ensure transparency and alignment around your organization's DEI objectives. And remember: this is not set in stone! Your purpose statement, like any business objective, might change over time, and that's okay.

3. **Audience**—Identify who is meant—and permitted—to look at this dashboard. Also specify who has the authority to expand the dashboard's visibility to others. If HR wants the business development team to see the dashboard, are they permitted to give that team access? Does permission have to come from the DEI team? The C-suite? Make sure this chain of command is clearly identified.

4. **Version and release notes**—Just as your business needs and objectives change over time, your dashboard is also likely to change over time. As this happens, keep track of updates through versioning and release notes.

5. **Refresh schedule**—How often you update the metrics in your DEI dashboard will depend on your infrastructure capabilities (How often can you collect the data? How often do the systems, which house the data, update?) and also your needs. If no one will be looking at the dashboard to perform daily tasks, you may not need to refresh it every day. To ensure your data remain relevant, however, we recommend updating at least monthly.

6. **Date/time last refreshed**—Anyone looking at your dashboard will need to know how up-to-date the data are, so make sure to include the date and time of when the data were last refreshed.

7. **Contact information**—If multiple people or groups will be looking at the dashboard, include contact information for the person or team responsible for managing it. This way everyone knows who to reach out to if they have a question, concern, or suggestion.

8. **Glossary (a.k.a "codebook")**—Last but not least, it's important to define your terms. In I-O psychology, we call this a "codebook," which is basically a glossary of all variables measured and what each value means (e.g., 1 = strongly disagree). A good set of codes, or definitions, helps everyone looking at the dashboard understand and interpret what they are seeing the same way.

Using the Dashboard

Once you've set up your dashboard, it's time to put it to use. You're finally ready to answer those DEI questions!

Learning from organizations with more advanced DEI data practices than our typical clients (who are more often at the beginning of their DEI journeys), we found that the way they use their dashboards has a lot to do with their specific business needs and DEI objectives. For instance, Bo Young Lee, chief diversity and inclusion officer at Uber, shared in a public webinar that people managers at Uber tend to have accelerated career trajectories. Therefore, Lee's team is working on getting more underrepresented individuals into those roles and tracking whether those individuals see correspondingly raised rates of career success at the company. Meanwhile, Michelle Wimes, the chief equity and inclusion officer at Children's Mercy Kansas City, said that her organization uses three different dashboards to track the three distinct populations that matter to the hospital. They use a supplier diversity dashboard to track how much business the hospital does with underrepresented vendors (and they set goals to increase those ratios over time). They use a health equity dashboard to determine whether patients with certain demographic characteristics are having better or worse outcomes than others (and adjust accordingly). And they are in the process of creating a workforce diversity dashboard in order to identify gaps in the hiring, promotion, and retention of underrepresented groups.

Regardless of business sector, everyone we interviewed told us that they use their dashboards not to identify endpoints, but to determine what questions to ask next. "Dashboards, if they're sliced right and nuanced enough, tell you quickly— ideally in real time—where to go to ask more questions," summarized Adam Murray of National Grid. The purpose of asking those follow-up questions is, of course, to take action: "If we see that the data is telling us that we're losing women by a 2 percent increase in downstate New York in this business unit, we're going to figure out what's going on and what decisions need to happen." Data is only as good as what you *do* with it.

Static Reports

If a dashboard is meant for tracking real-time data and delving deeper into specific issues as they arise, a static report provides a time-bound snapshot of the data at one moment in time and the insights gleaned from it. Unlike the dashboard, these are nearly always meant for broad distribution.

There are numerous reasons an organization may want to distribute a DEI report,[22] but the overarching motivation generally falls into one or more of the following categories:

1. To build trust through transparency. No one likes to be kept in the dark. Especially if they're being asked to contribute their time and attention to an initiative, employees want to see what has been found and what will be done based on those findings.

2. To demonstrate action is being taken. You can do all the DEI work you want behind the scenes, but perception, in many cases, is reality. If employees perceive nothing is being done about a DEI problem (especially if they provided input about that problem), related issues like attrition and lack of engagement may persist, and you can bet that these individuals won't be eager to help with your future data collection efforts. Moreover, there is increasingly more and more pressure from external stakeholders (e.g., customers, shareholders) for organizations to invest in DEI and show results. Sharing progress made toward DEI goals externally will make this work part of your brand and public reputation, which in turn will likely lead to attracting more customers, stakeholders, and even jobseekers.

3. To alert employees to interventions that they may witness or be asked to participate in. By giving advanced notice, offering the "why" behind the intervention, and supporting that "why" with data, organizations have a better chance of gaining employee support and participation in future DEI initiatives.

---

22 Brainstorm what a DEI report for *your* organization could look like by completing Worksheet #9 of the Inclusalytics Workbook, available at www.inclusalytics.com/workbook

Data Transparency

We believe all three reasons for sharing a DEI report are equally valid, and we encourage being as open and transparent about DEI work—including the data behind it—as possible. To this end, we recommend sharing some form of DEI output with all internal and external stakeholders of an organization. Doing this can be scary for many executives, but it adds a valuable layer of accountability.

However, as we see with our clients, different organizations treat data sharing differently. Fear—of litigation, of bad PR, of decreased morale—often prevents senior leaders from being fully transparent about every DEI finding they uncover. And every employee doesn't necessarily need (or want) to see every little thing. This is why it's important to be strategic about what ends up in the final report. However, if you are engaging certain groups of employees to help with improving **diversity**, **equity**, and/or **inclusion**, then they need to see more detailed data relevant to the issue they're being asked to address.

Sharing the data helps keep the momentum going. Not only can the **employee resource groups (ERGs)** see how their efforts are leading to more diversity, equity, and inclusion, they can use the data shared with them to further identify opportunities to better leverage DEI programming to reach the company's DEI goals.

Reporting Best Practices

Regardless of how much or how little you choose to share in a report, there are some best practices to follow. These are the four we consider most important.

Start with Key Takeaways

Most people—even those who are extremely invested—will never read an entire DEI report. Therefore, you want to start the report with what we're calling the *key takeaways* (also referred to as the "executive summary"). If a reader reads only one page of the report, what do you want them to know?

Short paragraphs and/or bullets are the most common ways to render what you want to share here: the most important findings from the data, what the organization is going to do about them, and (if applicable) what individuals can or will be asked to do. If the report is being presented to a specific audience, tailor the takeaways to the expertise of that audience. For example, if we are presenting to a team of **I-O psychologists** or statisticians, we will include more statistical details in the executive summary. If we are presenting to an entire organization, we'll stick to simpler percentages and visuals. (For the sake of transparency, however, we always include full details in our appendices so that anyone can delve deeper if they wish.)

As Mark Twain is alleged to have said, "Facts are stubborn things, but statistics are pliable." In other words, numbers can appear to be objective, but anyone who works with them knows that they can be manipulated. For example, look at these two graphs that show the same data but use different scales:

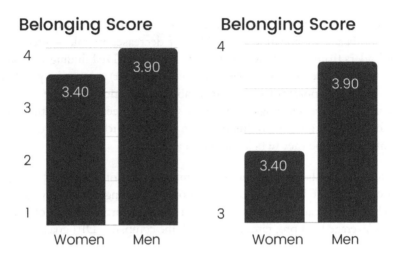

Figure 13

Therefore, it's our strong recommendation to always share your methods of data collection and analysis publicly. Like a scientist publishing their findings, you want whoever reads your report to understand what you did so they know how to interpret your findings and conclusions. You don't want to look like you have anything to hide, and you might even get some unexpected suggestions for other analyses you can add or tweak in the future!

That being said, not everyone will want to read about your methods, so you need to consider your audience. In a report to those who are more statistics-minded, it would make sense to share fairly detailed methods near the beginning of the report—they will want to know how and why you did what you did straightaway. In a report being distributed to a broader audience, on the other hand, it's probably best to present a simplified, abbreviated version of the methods up front and move the full description to an appendix at the back.

Rely on Visuals

Compared to key takeaways and methods, results are going to comprise the bulk of any DEI report. While you can share them in a number of different ways, the most direct and concise way we've found is to use visuals: bar graphs, line graphs, Venn diagrams. . . . The options are limitless. A picture (or in this case, a "figure") really is worth a thousand words.

Look at the graph example here:

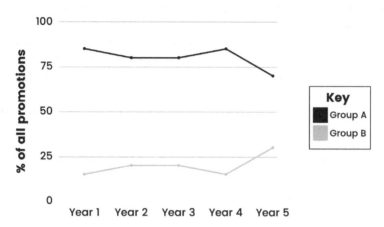

Figure 14

Did you need us to tell you that in year 5, we found that 30 percent of promotions went to group A, verses 70 percent of promotions going to group B? Probably not. The percentages are helpful, but you understood the take-home message—that group A is consistently being promoted at a lesser rate than group B—from the figure.

"It's amazing the impact that that can have on decision-making, because it's simple enough to understand," Lindsay Ciancetta said about using charts and graphs in DEI reporting. "It's powerful when you put it into that visual."

Select Meaningful Benchmarks

In our example graph, we showed a gap that our fictional DEI team uncovered at its fictional company. If that team were to report on that same metric next year, the most obvious benchmark to show whether the company had made progress on closing that gap would be the 2021 data. Are the promotion rates for groups A and B closer together or farther apart in 2022 than they were in 2021?

This sort of internal self-benchmarking is meaningful for many DEI initiatives, particularly those related to inclusion. However, sometimes external benchmarks make more sense, especially for diversity initiatives. If your organization is 10 percent Black, that statistic doesn't have any real meaning on its own. However, if you compare it against the entire US workforce (14 percent Black), or local demographics (22 percent Black in, say, New York City), now you might see that you have a problem. If what you're really trying to do is make your workforce representative of the local community, self-benchmarking won't cut it; you have to compare to an external measure.

Beyond the Report: Have a Communications Plan

Reports are great, but only if they actually get into the hands of the intended audience. In fact, distributing DEI results is so important that many organizations (Uber, Intel, Google—the list goes on) have created dedicated, public-facing DEI landing pages that are akin to a good DEI report—They share recent data, what's been done (internally and externally), and what will be done moving forward.

But reports, whether they're shared on paper or across the internet, are only one part of what has to be a more comprehensive DEI communications plan.

What Story Are You Telling?

Given that we've written this book, we clearly think data are fundamental to advancing DEI. Data reveal gaps, prove or disprove assumptions and hypotheses, and point out the direction an organization needs to take to be more diverse, equitable, and inclusive. However, when it comes to changing attitudes and beliefs—and, eventually, behaviors—you need a good narrative.

"Data has never changed someone's mind," said Bo Young Lee of Uber. "We use data as a mechanism to show people where we are; but then we use a form of narrative storytelling to paint the full picture, to appeal to not only people's brains but to their emotional side that drives behavior."

Stories can be leveraged in a variety of ways. One important way is to amplify the voices of the underrepresented groups whose experience you are trying to improve, particularly when progress is being made. Doing this helps those individuals to feel valued, respected, seen, and heard, and it can have a greater impact on others who identify with them or allies wanting to better understand and serve certain populations.

These days, the phrase "amplifying voices" has come to feel a bit generic, so here's an example of what we mean: after helping one of our clients roll out a new Black ERG, they collected feedback from their Black employees who attended the kickoff event. Two noteworthy responses were:

> *We're all energized by the reception to this effort. Today was an example of that. It had the indications of a watershed event in that there was a buildup of experiences and emotions, and the session provided a cathartic release for many people.*

> *The meeting was awesome. It brought me to tears to see all of the young Black professionals. The eagerness and the energy that was exhibited during the meeting was heartfelt and uplifting.*

This is very encouraging feedback, and we were pleased to hear it. The words are heartfelt, they stir emotion, and they may serve to encourage other, more hesitant peers to "buy into" and engage with the ERG. Such quotes can also signal to executives and other key DEI decision makers that investing in this ERG is already having a positive effect on Black employees. Therefore, these responses can be made even more impactful by sharing them with others as part of a broader communication effort.

Buy-in is equally important for the overrepresented group, and stories can help here as well. They don't even need to be "real" stories! Hypotheticals can work just as well. When we're trying to help men understand how a woman might feel being "the only" in a room or situation, we'll ask if the men have ever been, or could imagine being, the only man at a baby shower. How would they feel? What would they do? Would their behavior remain "normal," or would they change it somehow?

Finally, senior leaders are no more immune to stories than anyone else. For them, we recommend crafting the narrative in terms of what legacy they want to leave behind. Paint the picture by showing where they are right now—using data, of course—and where they could one day be when it comes to building a workplace where people from all backgrounds and identity groups have the opportunity to thrive. Tell other companies'—especially competitors'—DEI success stories. Build the narrative into your DEI report and encourage senior leaders to share their own aspirational DEI stories. The more leaders that can own the vision or "story" of what they want to achieve with DEI at their organization, the stronger their commitment will be and the greater the likelihood of success.

Always Share the Big Picture

An important part of DEI storytelling is telling the whole story. "What has been found" and "what is being done" are important elements, but connecting those two with a clear "why" is what makes the difference.

Lori McDonald, the CEO of Brilliance Business Solutions, gave a great example of sharing not only the *what* and the *how*, but also the *why* of a DEI initiative she undertook with her employees. When she first started centering DEI work at Brilliance, one of the initial elements she looked at was diversity. In comparing the demographic makeup of her eighteen employees to that of the surrounding area (a meaningful benchmark!), the biggest gaps that stood out were the disparities in Black and **Latiné representation**. "At first I thought maybe I shouldn't even be looking at this because we're relatively small; maybe only big organizations look at this," she said. But she realized that addressing these gaps now, before the company grew any bigger, would help to establish the right precedent for an inclusive culture.

One of the company's strategic goals was to hire eight new employees over the next two years. To work toward better representation of the surrounding community, she specifically targeted Black and Latiné candidates for these roles. Importantly, she shared these hiring targets—*and the reason for them* (the representation gap)—with the entire company at their annual kickoff meeting. "We need our teams to reflect the communities we're in," she told them. "When we were first looking into DEI work, we all said, 'We don't need to do this because we're really nice.' But it doesn't work that way."

Ciancetta said that she follows the same practice of sharing high-level DEI strategies to various stakeholders:

> *Here's everything we're working on; here's the clear delineation of the strategies, initiatives we're working on, where we're at with them, status updates. It doesn't have to be crazy in-depth, but you need your people to understand you are working, you're making progress, and you will continue to be as transparent as possible.*

Frequency and Variety Matter

Finally, if you're trying to tell a story that will ultimately influence behavior, you're going to need to tell it many times, in many ways. The best way to do this is to take a page out of the advertising playbook. (After all, advertisers are trying to influence behavior, too!)

In advertising, research shows that a potential customer will need to interact with a brand seven times before they make a purchase. That doesn't mean seven exposures to the same Instagram ad—in fact, seeing seven identical ads on the same platform in short succession might annoy a customer and dissuade them from purchasing. It means a TV ad, a product review, an email, a mention from a friend, an online banner, a Google search result, and a billboard, probably over the course of days, weeks, or even months. Your DEI communications plan should be similar.

"One of the critical things we've implemented this year is an internal communications plan where we are informing our ninety-two-plus employees on a regular basis—right now it's monthly—about the existence of the supplier diversity and inclusion program," said George Robinson II, the director of supplier diversity & inclusion at University of Pittsburgh Medical Center. "New individuals we've never had communications or contact with within our organization are now coming to supplier diversity saying, 'Hey, we saw your video; we saw this article on the internal publication; we've seen your external communications, whether radio or TV; how do we play our part?'"

That's the power of a multipronged communication plan. Be creative in how you communicate your message. Use multiple mediums, multiple platforms, and multiple messengers. Use written, visual, and video/auditory communications. And use them frequently. The more that DEI becomes a part of your organization's everyday vocabulary, the easier it will be to obtain cooperation and support for what we're about to discuss next: interventions.

PART III:

DATA-DRIVEN INTERVENTIONS: TURN INSIGHTS INTO ACTIONS

CHAPTER 10:
Build the Strategic Foundation

You might not realize it, but if you're following the methodology we've laid out thus far, you're ahead of the **DEI** curve. Most organizations set their DEI strategy first, then collect the data, then monitor changes over time. In this book, we have flipped those first two elements: we're collecting the data first and *then* developing the strategy. This is a more rigorous, scientific approach. We're letting the data inform the strategy we create, rather than looking for data that *backs up* the strategy we already set.

By now you have the data, the analyses, and your report(s) in hand, which means you're ready to move on to strategy. It's time to build the data-driven foundation for making changes to improve **diversity**, **equity**, and **inclusion** in your organization.

Setting the Strategy

As you review your data, there are several questions you can use to guide your strategizing. They pertain to organizational readiness, desired impact, level of intervention, setting benchmarks, and accountability.

"How ready is our organization for the changes we want to pursue?"

There are innumerable interventions an organization can deploy, and it will be impossible to tackle them all. Therefore, you need to focus on which will be most effective and impactful for *your* organization. One way to make those determinations is to evaluate where your organization is when it comes to DEI "maturity" or "readiness."

A DEI **Readiness Model** (also sometimes called a "maturity model") arranges organizational attributes in a way that indicates how prepared the organization is to adopt a given group of DEI interventions. (See Figure 15) In simpler terms: you need to walk before you can run, and if you can't even tie your shoes, don't start walking yet. There are plenty of models out there, but since this is our book, we're going to share our DEIx™ Organizational Readiness Model.

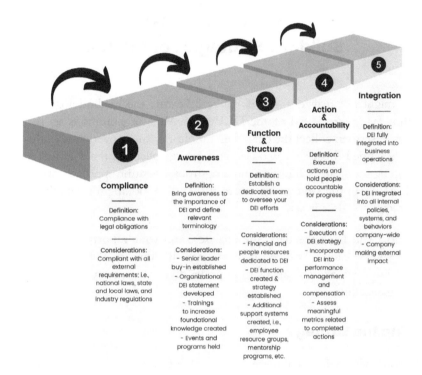

Figure 15

It's easiest to present this model linearly, to show how an organization "climbs the ladder." It's not a perfect **representation** because some interventions cut across rungs. For instance, education is ongoing, but while you are educating people, you're also performing actions such as ensuring they completed a mandatory **bias** training (Level 1) or measuring some training-driven behavior change as part of their performance management process (Level 4). (Conversely, if someone is scoring low on inclusive behaviors during performance evaluations, you may task them with completing extra training to increase their awareness.). But the general idea is that if you meet all the criteria on a lower rung, your organization is ready to climb up to the next rung. The important thing to understand is that as an organization progresses from one stage to the next, it's not only performing actions ("checking boxes"), but its culture is changing, as well. Progress can be measured by surveying your organization and asking employees questions to get their perspective on how you're doing.

INCLUSALYTICS CALLOUT

Below are some sample survey items you could use to gauge your organization's readiness:

- **Compliance:** "Our organization goes above and beyond legal requirements with their DEI efforts."
- **Awareness:** "People at our organization consistently use inclusive language."
- **Function & Structure:** "We have a well-resourced DEI team and a full-time leader of this group."
- **Action & Accountability:** "Our recruiters are required to actively seek out diverse talent when recruiting."
- **Integrated:** "Our organization applies a DEI lens to everything we do, including products and services."

We want to stress: *it is totally okay to be in any stage.* You are where you are. The key is to be able to recognize and own it! Identifying your organization's DEI readiness or maturity level is itself a form of **Inclusalytics**—you need to measure where you are now to determine where you need to go and how you're going to get there. Some companies bring in outside consultants to do a comprehensive DEI audit of all aspects of the organization and how they either support or deter DEI efforts— like an even more robust version of the **equity audit** we discussed in Chapter 5. Regardless of how you assess your organizational readiness, what's most important is knowing where you are so you then know where to *go* from there.

The first stage of our DEIx™ Readiness Model is *compliance.* When an organization is operating here, it's doing things because they are required, most often by the law. Remember our discussion of **adverse impact** in Chapter 8? That's a perfect example of a legal mandate that drives certain elements of DEI work. In the compliance stage, organizations are reacting to external forces such as changes in the law or pressure from shareholders.[1] Outside of compliance, if DEI interventions are proactively put in place, they are almost exclusively intended to improve diversity at the hiring stage, with little or no work being done on the inclusion side of the equation after those individuals are hired.

---

1   One example is the civil rights case of *Bostock v. Clayton County, Georgia,* in which the Supreme Court ruled that the Civil Rights Act of 1964 protects employees against discrimination because they are gay, lesbian, or transgender.

The second stage of our readiness model is *awareness*. At this stage, senior leaders understand the business case for DEI and have committed to doing whatever is necessary to advance DEI goals at their organization. DEI events are being held to raise awareness of the importance of DEI and to inform employees about the direction the organization is headed. Additionally, DEI training programs are being developed and implemented to teach every member of the organization about the prevalence of DEI issues, the importance of solving them, and actions an individual can take to contribute to a more inclusive culture. We'll discuss DEI training in greater depth in Chapter 12, but for now, just know that these trainings are neither one-size-fits-all nor one and done, and ongoing measurement needs to be done around participation, behavior change, and impact. Effective DEI training has a lot more to it than is often believed!

The third stage is *function and structure*. This is the stage at which an organization has really embedded DEI work into its core people operations. A DEI function—whether that's a DEI executive, team, or department—has been set up and defined. This function reports to the C-suite, has been given the budget, resources, and authority to develop a robust (data-driven!) DEI strategy, and is executing on that strategy. In addition, structures and practices have been put in place that enable employees to engage with and contribute to DEI efforts. This could mean setting up ally and **sponsorship** programs to help historically disadvantaged groups excel within the organization. It could also mean forming **employee resource groups (ERGs)** to elevate the voices and needs of underrepresented groups. (We'll discuss both of these interventions in greater depth in Chapter 13.) The key to this stage is firmly establishing DEI as something the organization truly values and prioritizes.

The fourth stage is *action and accountability*. Now an organization is confident enough in its DEI positioning to work toward changing everyday behaviors of its workforce. Starting at the very top, leaders and managers are made accountable for diversity targets and inclusive behaviors in concrete, measurable ways. Processes that form the foundation of the organization, from recruitment to hiring, training, and retention, are being consistently analyzed and reformed to improve diversity, equity, and inclusion for all. And, importantly, there is a robust system of measurement in place that is ongoing and feeds back into the organization's DEI and overall business strategies.

Stage four is one of the most uncomfortable stages of readiness because it's when the consequences of *not* getting on board with DEI get very real. These consequences must be both tangible and visible—felt and seen. They also must be standardized so that they apply across the organization, and everyone needs to be prepared to follow through on them. One example of this type of consequence-driven accountability is a zero-tolerance policy. Policies whereby anyone who exhibits **discrimination**, intimidation, or violence—especially toward individuals from marginalized groups—will be let go are not new. What is new, though, is that companies are actually enforcing them, even for leaders who may have previously been viewed as beyond reproach. Past offenses that were previously swept under the rug are now no longer acceptable.

We saw this play out with two of our clients when each had a senior executive publicly use an inexcusable racial slur. The first client investigated straightaway and fired the executive within days. The incident was still a blow to the company's culture, but that effect paled in comparison to the damage done by the second client, who took months to fire the guilty executive. In the latter case, the damage was so severe that the very few leaders who belonged to the most affected marginalized group left the organization—meaning that the higher-level diversity that company had worked so hard to achieve over the years was wiped out in a few months' time. Those are the stakes and why accountability and action must go hand in hand.

The fifth and final stage of readiness is *integration*. "But wait," you're probably saying, "I thought DEI was integrated into policies and practices by stage three!" You are correct—proactive DEI efforts are integral to an organization's *people* strategy at stage three, and they become more and more embedded throughout every aspect of the organization during stages four and five. The integration we're talking about here is the integration of DEI strategy and efforts into an organization's overarching operations, its market reach, even how products and services are designed and delivered.[2] It's the move from internal DEI to external DEI whereby the organization takes a DEI approach to everything it does. At this stage, the organization has moved its efforts beyond singular internal processes and is influencing the market in which it operates.

One final note on readiness: just because an organization progresses from one stage to the next does not mean the efforts it was making in a prior stage are "finished." Our readiness model builds on itself, with confidence in a given stage indicating a readiness to *add* the goals of the next stage. And stage five is not the end! Many organizations have lost ground due to complacency; even a simple change in leadership can shift an organization off its DEI course. That's why you'll hear us repeat this message again and again: you must continually monitor, measure, and iterate! DEI work is not a mountain to summit; it's an infinity loop with data propelling it ever forward.

---

2   Check out Annie Jean-Baptiste's book, *Building for Everyone*, to learn more about inclusive design.

"What impact do we want our intervention(s) to have?"

While this may seem like an obvious question to ask, it can easily get lost in the excitement over the intervention itself. We see this happen all the time with different types of trainings: an organization hears a sales pitch, gets excited about a particular training program, and puts their workforce through it . . . all without a concrete idea of what they were hoping the training would achieve. This lack of purpose often leads to disappointment and "wasted" money.

When choosing an intervention, whether a single tactic or a whole program, always start with your desired end state. What is it you want to see change? Are you trying to change people's attitudes and behaviors, or build people's knowledge about certain DEI topics? What organizational-level changes are you hoping to achieve? Be as specific as possible. Answering these questions not only helps you choose the intervention that will best yield the outcome you want, it also will tell you what you need to measure. Whatever it is you want to see change, that's what you need to measure.

"What's the right level to intervene?"

Part of achieving the impact you desire is choosing an intervention that affects the "right level" of an organization. This harkens back to the question of readiness: if the C-suite isn't ready to model inclusive leadership behaviors, then there is no reason to train others lower in the organization, because the behaviors aren't likely to stick.

Some of the most effective yet trickiest-to-implement interventions target middle management. "The population in the middle is the backbone of the org," said a senior DEI strategy, programs & analytics manager at an American energy corporation. Middle managers have, arguably, the most significant combination of responsibility and workload—they're responsible for operations getting done, but they also have the most immediate influence on how their team members experience the workplace. As they put it, "Middle managers are in the trenches every day."

Ultimately, because of the pressures middle managers are under and the workload they're managing, DEI cannot feel like an "extra task" they have to somehow find the time to complete. They don't have time for "extra tasks." Yet DEI is something they *must* prioritize if the organization is going to change. DEI work has to be embedded into how managers work every day. This is where some data collection could help not only increase the likelihood of implementation success, but also gain crucial buy-in from middle managers. Consider collecting some **qualitative data** (see Chapter 7 for a refresher) by asking middle management how an intervention would fit into their complex workday or if they have ideas for an intervention that would work better than whatever is being proposed. Design for your end-users!

Getting these managers on board also means helping them understand "What's in it for me?" The message to convey is that if they invest in their people—all of their people—they'll get workers who are highly engaged, loyal, and motivated to bring their best selves to work each day. Middle managers need the education and support to understand that doing the DEI work will, in the long run, make their lives easier.

"What goals should we set?"

The question of setting targets, or "meaningful benchmarks," ties back to our discussion in Chapter 9. If you want to make progress on a DEI measure, you need to know not only where you're starting and what you want to see change, but also *how much* change you're shooting for.

When it comes to setting diversity goals, representation is key. Three benchmarks to look at are national averages, local demographics, and the market or industry within which you operate. Let's use recruitment as an example. To set hiring targets for a given demographic group, you could use national averages from sources such as the Bureau of Labor Statistics. These data reveal how many people in your labor market—broken into demographic groups—have the prerequisites to be successful in the job for which you are hiring.

Another option is using industry-specific averages to set diversity goals. However, one caveat: industry-specific data provide a snapshot of where the industry currently is, not necessarily where we want it to be. For example, women hold only about 24 percent of senior-level roles in tech. A company seeing this stat may set it as a benchmark and feel "done" once they hit 20 percent women in tech roles. However, women comprise about 50 percent of the world population. We therefore argue that 50 percent female representation is what organizations should strive to achieve, across all leadership levels. This is why we prefer using geographic population data over industry-specific data—it gives us more aspirational goals.

To this end, you can look at the areas where your organization operates and the client base you serve. Hospitals and health providers in particular are growing more sensitive to this benchmark. When examining their workforce and patient demographics, Adeola Oduwole, the chief equity, diversity and inclusion officer at Ann & Robert H. Lurie Children's Hospital of Chicago found that "there is almost zero congruence between what our providers look like and what our patients look like. Because they couldn't see themselves in those who provided them care, it was no surprise that patient satisfaction was lower among nonwhite patients—they didn't feel like they belonged. Now that the hospital has these data in hand, it is working on DEI strategies to close this gap.

Your competitors can also help you set DEI goals. Just make sure to account for differences like size and budget. George Robinson II described accounting for these differences his work on supplier diversity for the University of Pittsburgh Medical Center (UPMC): a competitor, Kaiser Permanente, spends $1 billion annually on diverse suppliers—four times more than UPMC spends ($250 million). (See Figure 16) So at a glance, it looks like UPMC has a lot of ground to make up. However, Kaiser's $1 billion spend is only 0.6 percent of the organization's total supplier budget, whereas $250 million is *7.5 percent* of UPMC's vendor budget. "So you have to put it in an apples-to-apples viewfinder," said Robinson. "When you compare where other healthcare providers are in our same category, we are a national leader."

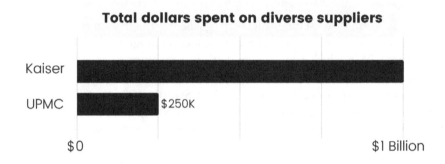

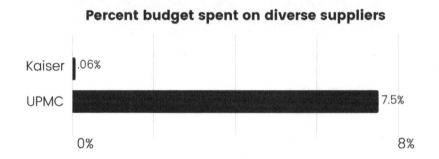

Figure 16

"Who will be held accountable?"

Last but not least, there is the question of accountability. If you hit the DEI benchmarks you're aiming for, who is rewarded? Or, if you fall short, who is held responsible?

Our recommendation is to take those **impact measures** you identified, roll them up under the broader benchmarks you're aiming for, and assign each one to a single leader. To repeat: a *single* leader is to be held accountable for a given KPI, not multiple leaders. Sure, DEI is often a team effort, but there should always be a single owner of every DEI goal. We've seen this mistake made time and time again: if you disperse accountability, no one is ultimately held accountable . . . which often results in nothing getting accomplished.

Generating Ideas

With your overarching strategy in place,[3] you can move on to choosing interventions. We're going to cover a number of evidence-based interventions in the coming chapters, but we want to stress that what we present is *not* an exhaustive list. In fact, rather than just choosing from our (or any) list of potential DEI interventions, you're better off getting ideas from within your own organization!

We had great success with the following idea-generating approach in our inclusive leadership workshops. In a recent example, our intention was to lead company executives through an exercise that would result in them generating their own action plan to integrate inclusive leadership into their everyday work and interactions with their teams. We began with some light education on what inclusion is (it's behavior change!). We then asked each executive to identify what the following, research-based, inclusive leadership behaviors looked like at their organization:

- Visible commitment (publicly prioritizing and pursuing—and holding others accountable for prioritizing and pursuing—DEI objectives)

- Humility (admitting mistakes and welcoming contributions from others)

- Awareness of bias (recognizing personal blind spots and flaws in the system)

- Curiosity about others (maintaining an open mindset and seeking to understand others)

- Effective collaboration (empowering others and fostering team cohesion)

- Cultural intelligence (recognizing and adapting to others' cultures)

---

3   Begin taking a more strategic approach to developing DEI interventions at *your* organization by completing Worksheet #10 of the Inclusalytics Workbook, available at www.inclusalytics.com/workbook

After that brainstorming session, we presented the baseline data (extracted from a recently completed employee **engagement** survey) that showed areas where leaders needed to improve in general, as well as gaps between different demographic groups. We then sent the executives into breakout rooms to come up with inclusive leadership behaviors they might use to move the needle in each of the targeted areas identified in the engagement survey data.

At the end, we consolidated everything into a one-page list of actionable next steps they could employ to improve employee engagement through leading more inclusively. The best part was that the executives came up with the specific actions themselves, making them more likely to actually use these behaviors in the future.

But executives aren't the only ones with actionable DEI-related ideas. Other leaders, managers, employees, and even customers are rich sources of data for potential interventions that can be applied "on the ground."

In 2019, National Grid hosted a two-day retreat called "Beyond the Metrics." At this retreat, which was attended by every senior leader in the organization (about 150 in all), attendees were grouped by business unit and tasked with personalizing their business's DEI goals. Each business unit receives a data pack containing diversity data and **qualitative data** from the previous year pertaining to that business. They spend the first half of that first day reviewing and analyzing the data. Then, they spend the remaining day and a half focusing on what the unit can do to create a more diverse, equitable, inclusive environment. When each group has identified what they want to do, the DEI team helps them to develop tools they can use to take action and track progress. "We hope to continue this exercise every few years to ensure that leaders are looking 'beyond the metrics' and moving towards action in their DEI journeys," said Adam Murray, the US director of diversity, equity, and inclusion at National Grid.

"We really try to individualize the approach to DEI for each business unit depending upon their needs, giving them metrics and dashboards that make sense for them. Sometimes that means a specific metric for that business unit and sometimes a DEI metric for the whole organization," said Adam Murray, the US director of diversity, equity, and inclusion. One business unit might be further along in their DEI journey and is ready to employ targeted DEI interventions, while another business unit could just be getting started and needs the foundational knowledge of what bias is and how it can lead to detrimental outcomes. The needs of these units, and the ideas they generate, will necessarily be different.

Gathering ideas can even be as simple as including an open-ended question on a survey. You never know where you'll find a great idea! An ice cream chain once did a **pulse survey** about improving company culture, and one of the responses said that because workers could only play one genre of music in their stores, it wasn't very inclusive to them *or* to their customers in that neighborhood. Senior leaders had never considered this perspective, so they updated their policy to let stores select their own music. That small corporate policy change radically improved the environment for many of the chain's employees and its customers. Plus, not only was the change effective, but it was also simple and essentially zero cost.

Beware the "Visibility Trap"

As you set your strategy and choose your interventions, we have one final word of warning: be careful not to fall into the "visibility trap."

Many organizations want to show that they're taking DEI seriously. There's nothing wrong with that. In fact, it's important to share the steps your organization is taking to close gaps between different identity groups and improve employees' and customers' overall experiences. A lack of transparency around these actions (and their results) will lead people to believe that DEI doesn't matter to the organization, even if it does. For instance, in **focus groups** we recently conducted for a client, a few participants complained that even though theirs was a female-dominated industry, most of the directors and senior leaders were male. However, when we presented this sentiment to the DEI team, they confirmed that the complaint was factually incorrect; the majority of directors and senior leaders were, in fact, female. The real issue was a lack of communication within the organization. Employees were unaware of the steps their organization had taken and the progress it had made in diversifying leadership and getting more women into top positions. This is why we recommend sharing regular status updates with your organization!

However, a lot of DEI interventions aren't going to *look* like DEI. For the client we just mentioned, DEI work meant partnering with their HR team to improve talent acquisition and retention processes for female leaders. Other less visible interventions can include seemingly innocuous changes like loosening a dress code or letting employees control the music in the stores where they work. These interventions can be a lot harder to hype up than the big-ticket speakers, the fancy training program, and other "showier" interventions. But if they result in a more inclusive and equitable environment, then they're important. Don't fall for choosing the higher-visibility DEI intervention over the more effective one.

That being said, the flashier intervention might really be the best choice. In that case, make sure you clearly communicate the strategy behind the intervention. Otherwise, you could be perceived as **virtue signaling**, also known as moral grandstanding, where individuals make a contribution that is motivated by recognition rather than making meaningful change. A number of organizations made this mistake during the resurgence of the Black Lives Matter movement in the summer of 2020. They were donating money right and left to support community organizations fighting for social justice, but when there was no clear strategy explained and no obvious follow-up, employees and customers began wondering, "Was all that donating **performative**? What did these companies actually *do*?"

INCLUSALYTICS CALLOUT

Be sure to communicate the impact of your various DEI efforts frequently and with hard numbers associated with the outcomes you see (or intend to see as a result of your efforts).

The Implementation Plan is Key

Poor communication around an intervention is one of the many reasons why you need to have an implementation plan in place *before* you start rolling out your interventions. Here's a more concrete illustration:

Imagine you're the head of DEI for a multimedia company, and you've identified that you have a diversity gap—say a dearth of Latina employees—that you want to close. You've also identified that part of the problem comes from your pipeline: there simply don't seem to be enough Latinas in broadcast media to even apply to open roles. Therefore, you decide to invest in local journalism and public speaking programs that explicitly serve Latina girls and women.

By publicly announcing what you're doing, you're signaling to the current, limited pool of Latina journalists that you're invested in this issue, which will (hopefully!) make them more likely to apply to your company. *However,* if your implementation plan doesn't include a communications campaign explaining the *full strategy* behind the monetary investment, it could backfire. Why? Because simply announcing that you've tossed money toward a "young Latinas in journalism" program can look performative. It needs a strong communications plan around it to signal to current employees and future applicants that this isn't a one-time Band-Aid approach and that you're invested in this issue in a meaningful way. You're in it for the long haul…and you may even get some short-term gains (i.e., more Latina applicants now) as well!

Hopefully from this illustration you can see that your *intervention* plan is only as good as your *implementation* plan. Strong implementation means partnering closely with your communications team, learning and development team, the executives who will sponsor and kick off the initiative, any external consultants or organizations with whom you are partnering, and any other key stakeholders. With all of these groups engaged, you can find the optimal time to launch your intervention (i.e., *not* during the organization's busiest season, like during the holidays if you're in retail), as well as the most effective way to inform—and then engage—managers, employees, contractors, and customers.

Developing an implementation plan will also help you to identify if you have sufficient in-house capacity to deliver—and measure!—your intervention effectively. If not, who or what will you bring in to help? Maybe you need a consulting team, or maybe you just need some Inclusalytics tools. Do you have the necessary budget for these things? If not, you may need to rescope and come back with a new plan.

Finally, don't forget to build in key performance metrics to assess your implementation plan. These can be as simple as the date by which a communications plan is written, reviewed, and signed off. Or the number of people who attend an ERG-sponsored event or the percentage of leaders who volunteer to be a part of a new DEI initiative. As you know by now, if you want to see if something's working, you need to be able to measure it. We've repeated this sentiment throughout the book, and it's one we're going to emphasize again in the next two chapters as we present the part of DEI work that often gets our clients most excited: interventions.

CHAPTER 11:
Attract & Retain a Diverse Workforce

With a data-driven strategy in place and all the necessary teams aligned, it's time to get going with **DEI** interventions. It bears repeating that the interventions we present in the next few chapters are not an exhaustive list. (That's why you need to ask your workforce for their ideas!) What we've chosen to include are some key evidence-based DEI interventions that we've researched and helped organizations put into practice. And because they are applicable to organizations at *every* stage of readiness, we're starting with DEI interventions that impact the recruitment, selection, and retention of people.

Recruitment

When it comes to improving **diversity** within an organization, the very first challenge is getting the candidates you want in the door. This process of improving your **talent pipeline**—that is, the pool of individuals who are qualified and prepared to step into roles at your organization when they fall vacant—can begin before someone is even ready to job hunt. It then extends all the way through to people who are already doing work for your organization, especially those high-performing employees who have the potential to climb to the highest levels of leadership.

For years, various leaders across industries have excused their organizations from pursuing fair, reflective workforce **representation** by protesting that "it's a pipeline issue." That excuse might have worked at one time, but it no longer holds water. Organizations that are serious about DEI must make it their responsibility to fix the pipeline issue, even if that means spending resources outside of the company to invest in diversifying your industry as a whole.[4]

---

4   Explore potential leaks in *your* organization's talent pipeline by completing Worksheet #11 of the Inclusalytics Workbook, available at www.inclusalytics.com/workbook

Early Skill Development

A long-term strategy for increasing the diversity in your pool of qualified candidates is working to develop needed skills in underserved populations *before* they enter the job market. It's sort of like farming versus foraging: foraging is quicker and easier in the short term, but you are limited to whatever happens to be available. Conversely, if you seed and nurture what you really want, with the right conditions and environment you eventually get to reap what you sow.

There are a number of ways you can "seed and nurture" a more diverse workforce. One way is to work with colleges and universities, particularly those that serve historically disadvantaged populations,[5] to inform students of postgraduation employment opportunities in your field (and even at your organization) when they are selecting their majors. This means you can have an impact as early as freshman year! You can also create apprenticeships and paid internships for underrepresented high school and college students. (We must put emphasis on *paid*, as unpaid internships are accessible only to those with the means to support themselves using other funds—a **privilege** often not available to those from historically disadvantaged groups.) This will help them to gain experience in your industry and develop relevant work skills while providing you with potential candidates whom you can vet in a low-risk environment. Tech companies in particular have even begun offering boot camps and training programs to develop diverse talent in-house, like IBM's SkillsBuild or Google's Career Certificate programs.

Of course, your organization doesn't need to stand up all of these programs itself. There are lots of groups out there already doing this work. Therefore, investing in programs that develop desirable talents and skills in underserved populations is a perfectly viable option. Start local and specific. For example, if you are a Pittsburgh-based company and have a gap in Black software engineers, partner with and invest in community organizations that are getting local Black youth interested in tech, such as Toyz Electronics and Black Tech Nation. National options include Black Girls Code or /dev/color.[6] Just be sure to clearly communicate the strategy behind making this investment both internally and externally.

---

5   These are collectively called Minority Serving Institutions and include Historically Black Colleges and Universities (HBCUs), Hispanic-Serving Institutions (HSIs), Tribal Colleges and Universities (TCUs), and Asian American and Pacific Islander Serving Institutions (AAPISIs).

6   Learn more about these organizations at https://www.blackgirlscode.com/ and https://devcolor.org/

Meanwhile, when an organization is clearly invested in fixing the talent pipeline for underrepresented groups, it signals to diverse talent in the market that this organization is serious about long-term DEI solutions. In turn, diverse talent will be more likely to apply to that organization. Playing the long game (improving the diversity of the talent pool) will help you simultaneously win the short game (getting more diverse applicants *now*)!

INCLUSALYTICS CALLOUT

Be sure to assess the ROI of various partnerships in fixing your representation issues. Which education programs have the most underrepresented alumni who end up in jobs or degree programs that will contribute to fixing the talent pipeline? Which boot camps are graduating the most people from historically disadvantaged groups?

Recruiting from Diverse Networks

Once you've analyzed your present candidate pool and identified diversity gaps to address, you need to ensure that your recruiting efforts extend to a variety of networks and not just the ones that yield the "most" candidates. After all, if "most" of your candidates have historically come from the overrepresented group, you're not going to increase the diversity of your hires by going back to the same sources.

To go beyond the most obvious or traditional talent sources, it can be helpful to look at some data. Here we specifically mean demographic data: if you need to hire employees to work in a physical location, look at the demographics of the surrounding neighborhoods and nearby towns to see where your target populations live. This will inform you of how you should concentrate your outreach efforts. Likewise, if you want to hire more entry-level employees with a certain set of credentials and demographic attributes—say, a first-year Asian lawyer—then you'll want to recruit from schools that enroll higher percentages of students with those backgrounds.

Also, consider leaving out the four-year university degree requirement entirely. The tech field is ahead of this curve, as evidenced by the growing number of boot camps that equip anyone with the necessary skills to enter the tech field. Assuming the roles you need to fill don't require specific degrees like JD or MD, look into acceleration programs that have a strong focus on **equity** (e.g., Apprenti) or local boot camps (e.g., The Hidden Genius Project in Oakland, CA).

Finally, merely having a presence at events or conferences that attract and serve diverse groups is an effective form of outreach. Being visible in these spaces demonstrates to prospective employees that you are working to be a part of their community and see value in gatherings that are designed to engage them. In effect, being visible matters. Go to where diverse talent is, rather than waiting for those individuals to come to you.

INCLUSALYTICS CALLOUT

When it comes to identifying which partnerships yield the most diverse applicants (and therefore which you want to continue to invest in), collecting data can be as simple as adding a "How did you hear about us?" item on your job application. But don't keep these data to yourself! Share your findings back with these sourcing groups so they have the opportunity to double down on what's working.

Recruiter and Employee Incentives

Reaching out to new, more diverse networks is an "organizational" behavior change. To get more diverse applicants into an organization, individuals need to change their behaviors, too.

One way to do this is through incentives. It's a normal practice to incentivize employees to recruit qualified candidates by offering referral bonuses or "finder's fees" if the candidate is hired. Intel has capitalized on this practice by doubling the referral bonus for staff who referred diverse candidates. Facebook, meanwhile, has tied staff recruiters' performance reviews and bonuses to the diversity of the candidates they recruit. While this hasn't yet improved the percentage of **Latiné** and Black employees working in US offices, it has contributed to increasing the number of female employees.

INCLUSALYTICS CALLOUT

If your organization chooses to adopt this approach, be sure to measure the pre–post difference in the number of referrals from underrepresented groups, leaving enough time (e.g., six or twelve months) for the intervention to have an effect.

Scrutinize Job Descriptions

So far we've talked about how to cultivate, find, and attract qualified applicants who can bring more diverse identities to your organization. The next intervention has to do with removing barriers that might discourage individuals from underrepresented groups from applying in the first place—specifically **biases** hidden within job descriptions.

Unconscious bias—also called "implicit bias"—is **prejudice** or unsupported judgments in favor of or against one thing, person, or group as compared to another. The word "unconscious" is key here, because it means we're not aware of these prejudices and judgments. That's what makes them so insidious and enables them to creep into elements of the hiring process, like job descriptions.

Perhaps the easiest change you can make to any job description is to get rid of requirements that don't actually matter to do the job. To use our earlier example: Is a four-year degree *really* required to be successful in the role you need to fill? Or does the person merely need skills like critical thinking and the ability to self-direct, which are often associated (because of biases) with earning a bachelor's degree? If the latter is true, scrap the degree requirement and replace it with those skills. Now you've opened the job up to individuals who otherwise would have been screened out!

This unnecessary elimination of qualified candidates is the reason Baltimore Tracks, a coalition committed to increasing opportunities for **BIPOC** in technology, gives for not requiring four-year degrees:

> *College degrees do not cause professional achievement exclusively, and so this commitment aims to challenge how we view "qualified candidates.". . . College is increasingly expensive and, as a result, requiring a college degree perpetuates a system wherein companies miss out on qualified candidates by selecting from a relatively small and privileged group of graduates.*

Given that as of 2017, only 17.3 percent of Latiné and 24.2 percent of Blacks aged twenty-five and older attained a bachelor's degree or higher, you're expanding your applicant pool quite a bit by eliminating the four-year-degree requirement.

With the requirements that remain, make sure you specify which are required to do the job versus which are "nice to have." Eliminate or severely limit the "nice to have" skills, as women in particular will self-select out of the applicant pool when they don't meet 100 percent of the requirements, whereas most men apply to roles if they merely meet at least 60 percent. Women will also be less likely to apply to a job if they encounter gendered language. Masculine-themed words such as "competitive" and "dominant" can affect perceptions of belongingness and consequently decrease the appeal of a job to more feminine-minded individuals. Likewise, words associated with female stereotypes, like "nurturing," may turn away more masculine applicants.

Of course, gender **bias** isn't the only type of bias that can creep into job descriptions. Ableism is another common one. How often is the office worker you're hiring *actually* going to lift an item that weighs twenty pounds? Meanwhile, language like "thrives in a bright, bustling, and energetic environment" can not only screen out candidates with unseen disabilities, such as hearing loss or migraines, but it also indicates a preference for younger candidates. Subtle ageism is in fact rampant in many industries, with terms like "tech savvy," "digital native," or "high energy" being code for "younger," while words like "seasoned" imply "older."

One way to screen for biased, exclusionary language is to solicit feedback from the people who would be most likely to be affected by it. **Employee resource groups (ERGs)**, which we'll discuss in more detail in the next chapter, are great for this. You can also A/B-test job descriptions; publish two versions and measure the demographic differences of candidates who apply via either description.

INCLUSALYTICS CALLOUT

There are a number of tech tools that can assist you in screening out bias from your job descriptions and other written language. Textio, Datapeople, TalVista, and Text Analyzer (by Ongig) are a few that can help identify language that is gendered, ageist, tokenistic, exclusionary, and/or inaccessible, and suggest alternative words or phrases.

Selection and Hiring

As you improve upon your recruitment strategies for reaching a more diverse pool of candidates, you'll also need to evaluate your selection and hiring processes. After all, getting more diverse applications is useful only if you ultimately hire the applicants!

Reducing Interviewer Bias

We just discussed unconscious bias in the context of job descriptions; however, that's not the end of the discussion. Like it or not, we all have unconscious biases, which means that, just like everyone else, interviewers are being affected by their unconscious biases in every interview they conduct.

Awareness of these biases is a great first step and is why there is so much unconscious bias training happening in organizations these days. Yet awareness does not equal mitigation, and bias mitigation is the name of the game if you want to bring in more diverse candidates who will excel in a role, not just "fill a quota." (It should go without saying, but we'll say it anyway: merely filling a diversity quota is *not* a good reason to hire someone. See the discussion of **tokenism** back in Chapter 2.)

The reason awareness of biases is insufficient to correct for them is that conscious bias suppression simply does not work. Numerous studies have demonstrated this, including one where business school students were tasked with evaluating job applications. Before they completed the task, they watched a diversity training video that instructed them to suppress negative stereotypes about elderly job applicants. The result? They actually evaluated the older applicants *more* negatively, not less.

If conscious bias suppression isn't the answer, we need to find systematic ways to negate bias that don't rely on an individual self-policing. One solution is to mask demographic features of applicants. A great example of this comes from orchestras: Back in 1970, only 5 percent of the musicians in America's top orchestras were women. The judges sitting in the auditions insisted they were only judging based on the quality of the music they heard. Yet when musicians began performing their auditions behind a screen—masking their identity entirely—the likelihood that a female musician would advance to the next round of auditions increased by 50 percent.[7] Today, women make up more than a third of orchestra membership.

We obviously can't put people's resumes behind a screen, but tools like "redacted resume review" from TalVista can create this same effect by blinding employers to applicants' personally identifiable information (e.g., name, email address) and details that would indicate demographic characteristics (e.g., headshots, schools/universities, dates). GapJumpers uses a similar "resume-blinding" methodology, but the resume review doesn't even come up until after a "blind audition." Applicants must anonymously first solve skills-based challenges in order to demonstrate that they possess the qualities and skills necessary to do the job they're applying for. This way, skills are emphasized and identity is de-emphasized—all with the goal of reducing bias while finding the best candidate for the role.

Another strategy is to adjust the interviewing process to remove some of the elements that may trigger interviewer bias. For instance, is a firm handshake essential to the job of a teacher? Most of us were probably taught that it's essential to nailing a job interview, but grip strength is unlikely to be important for teaching high schoolers history or calculus. What this handshake can do, however, is unintentionally screen out autistic candidates who are hypersensitive to touch but otherwise possess all the skills needed for that teaching job. Or women who may not have as firm of a grip compared to men. As with the job description,

---

7   In fact, orchestra auditions only saw this 50 percent increase after they *required musicians to take off their shoes* before walking onstage. Even behind the curtain, the women were still being identified (and implicitly discriminated against) because judges could hear their high heels on the floor (Goldin & Rouse 2000).

look for and attempt to strip away elements of your interview process that may lead to biased outcomes based on information unrelated to the job. (As fun as it is to bond with a candidate over a shared alma mater or love of the same sports team, this information is unnecessary and can trigger bias!)

INCLUSALYTICS CALLOUT

Assess adverse impact (as discussed in Chapter 8) and identify any other ways you can use data to evaluate the impact of your organization's hiring practices on DEI goals. (Remember, these can be positive or negative impacts—be sure to look for both.) Measure if you are seeing an increase in diversity in your selection data after implementing any changes.

Reducing Stereotype Threat

If unconscious bias can keep an interviewer from hiring more diverse candidates, **stereotype threat** has a similarly negative effect on the interviewee.

Over the past few decades, a number of studies have been conducted around stereotype threat—which, as we described in Chapter 2, is the self-fulfilling prophecy whereby an individual fears that their behaviors will be perceived as fulfilling a negative stereotype about their group and, consequently, they act accordingly. The research has shown that immediate surroundings can change people's mindsets in ways that prevent them from performing to their full potential. For instance, something as simple as being in a math class filled with predominantly men can trigger the stereotype "Women are bad at math." The effect is that women score lower on a math test in that men-filled room than if they took the test in a room with more equal or even female-dominant representation. The truth is that women *aren't* bad at math, as evidenced by the higher test scores in environments where they are not the minority. Women in a roomful of men just fall victim to the self-fulfilling prophecy that they're bad at math because of stereotype threat . . . regardless of their actual math ability.

You can see how this would create a problem for hiring: if you're hiring for a residency program in a hospital and all of the Black candidates are performing poorly in their interviews, then of course you won't hire them. Yet if the interview is conducted in a room decorated with photos of only non-Black graduates, or if an interviewer mentions affirmative action as a means to recruit faculty from underrepresented groups, then you're creating the same situation as the study: stereotype threat—In this case the stereotype "Black people are not as smart as white people"—is likely causing your Black candidates to underperform.

Researchers King and Gilrane (2015) suggest two solutions. One is to provide access to a positive group role model. This can be done by sharing an example of an underrepresented employee who has been successful at the organization, or even having them in the room. Kellie Molin Kénol, global head of diversity, equity & inclusion at the global pharmaceutical company Endo International, says that this is an approach they've taken. "We have mandated diverse interview panels. We try our best to include at least two BIPOC individuals and one woman on every panel." (More on **panel interviews** shortly.)

The other strategy for reducing stereotype threat is to prompt applicants to think of qualities outside of the stereotyped area via a question or written assignment. This, in essence, "distracts" them from focusing on the negative stereotype and instead directs their attention to an area of strength. This could be as simple as taking a negative-leaning question like "Describe a time when you failed" and using **positive presuppositions**—framing a statement or question to presume positive intent—to reframe it as "Describe a time when you applied what you learned from a previous mistake."

INCLUSALYTICS CALLOUT:

Send a candidate experience survey to all interviewees asking them questions such as, "Overall, how was the interview process? Did you feel like we prepared you for the interview? Did you feel like you could be your authentic self in the interview?" Compare subgroup differences to assess if your interview process favors some groups over others.

Increasing Fairness of Evaluations

At this point we've gone over the "people" side of the hiring equation, so what remains are the processes and procedures. The fairer, clearer, more transparent, and more accurate you can make any part of your evaluation process, the more likely you will be to successfully increase the diversity of your new hires.

The first thing to do is to make sure that any tests or evaluations mimic the job's actual requirements as closely as possible. This sounds obvious, but you'd be amazed at how often the "easy-to-administer" test is chosen over the one that most closely matches the job experience. Choosing the former over the latter can unintentionally screen out candidates who might otherwise be a great fit. For instance, a candidate who doesn't have great written English language skills would struggle to take a written test. However, if the job they're applying for doesn't require writing (like a manufacturing job), then a video-based or orally administered test would provide a much more accurate representation of whether they possess the skills they need for the job. The same goes for complex, high-pressure "gotcha"-type questions (like, "How many golf balls would fill Yankee Stadium?"): if it's not something the candidate will face in their day-to-day work, there's no reason to use it as a screening measure. Trick questions are a waste of everyone's time.

Another way to increase fairness in the hiring process is to standardize interviews by using a format called a **structured interview**. Structured interviewing is a practice whereby every interviewee receives the same set of questions in the same order. Interviewers use a rubric of criteria that is consistently applied to each candidate and score their answers in real time. Research has shown that structured interviews decrease differences between demographic groups and increase fairness for diverse groups of candidates. And if that's not enough for you, Google—a company that has spent a significant amount of time and money figuring out how to hire top talent—has found structured interviews to be better predictors of job performance than unstructured interviews.

One warning about structured interviews: they sometimes feel *too* scripted, or even cold. To avoid this, make the interviewee aware of the process. This helps them understand the purpose behind what you are doing and will help prevent their walking away having had a poor overall candidate experience—which could result in their self-selecting out of the applicant pool and detrimentally affecting your diversity goals.

Another interviewing process that has a positive effect on diverse hiring is panel interviews. A **panel interview** is simply an interview that includes multiple interviewers, usually three to five. Panelists may include the potential manager, colleagues, or other coworkers who would have frequent interaction with the candidate if they got the job. This collection of individuals should be diverse in order to reduce bias while signaling to the candidate that they belong. As an added bonus, panel interviews also create an opportunity to see how a candidate handles group dynamics and, when done effectively, speeds up the interview process. However, if your organization currently has only a few employees from underrepresented groups, be careful not to burden them with sitting on every single hiring panel. Additionally, it's important for each interviewer on the panel to take their own notes and submit their own ratings before talking to each other; this helps to avoid "**groupthink**" (interviewers' opinions influencing each other).

Last but not least, make your interviewing process as transparent as possible—namely, what can and cannot be negotiated. Research has shown that men are more likely than women to negotiate salary and that this contributes to the wage gap. However, in a randomized control trial of twenty-five hundred MBA students seeking their first job, researchers found that when applicants were clearly informed that wages were negotiable, women *and* men were equally likely to negotiate and equally hesitant to offer working for lower wages.

Talent Retention

So, you've increased the diversity of your applicants, they've shown themselves to be a good fit, and they're now full-time employees. Congratulations! But the work is far from done. You got these employees in; now you need them to stay.

A huge part of getting employees to stay is making them feel like they belong. We're going to cover that side of the retention equation in the next chapter. (**Inclusion**—which yields **belonging**—is both crucial and multifaceted, which is why interventions gets its own chapter.) For the remainder of this chapter, we're going to cover some of the more equity-focused interventions; because if you aren't treating your underrepresented employees equitably, they're not going to stay.

Compensation: Closing the Wage Gap

A problem many organizations uncover at the beginning of their DEI journey is a wage gap. Sometimes not just one. In 2021, McKinsey & Company estimated that a $220 billion annual wage disparity exists between Black and white workers in America, with Black workers underrepresented in higher-paying occupations and paid less, on average, than white workers in the same roles. Meanwhile, women still make only $0.82 for every dollar earned by a man, with that gap widening even further when factors like race and age—i.e., **intersectionality**—are factored in.

Now remember: when we talk about a wage gap, we are talking about a pay discrepancy between two employees who possess equivalent experience and expertise; the only difference is a demographic one. If you discover this sort of gap at your organization, you need to find a way to fix it. One way is to stop asking applicants for their previous salary or their desired salary. If you can shift to paying applicants what they're worth rather than "what you can get them for," you'll make real progress toward improving pay equity within your organization. Of course, this method affects only incoming applicants; it will help close the gap among new employees but not your current workforce (which, with the exception of quickly growing startups, likely comprises the vast majority of your overall organization).

To close the gap *now*, you could adjust payroll for *all* employees. This is what Salesforce did back in 2015 (and virtually every year thereafter). By externally sharing the investment they are making in pay equity to level the playing field among their employees, the company has received what amounts to a free pro-equity publicity campaign to stakeholders, including future diverse applicants. (Of course, that's assuming you can call spending millions more dollars on payroll "free.") Salesforce is positioning itself as a more attractive place for women and other historically underrepresented people to work, and it's making sure that if these populations do leave the company, it's not for lack of fair pay.

INCLUSALYTICS CALLOUT

We mentioned pay equity analysis in Chapter 5. This can be as simple as comparing the average pay of individuals from different groups or as complex as conducting a regression analysis, which would allow you to control for additional variables such as experience or job level. Beware, however, that even simple pay equity analyses come with a number of factors to consider, including legal requirements. Fortunately, there are a number of tools and vendors, such as DCI Consulting,[8] available to assist you with this huge Inclusalytics undertaking.

Opportunities and Promotions

Understandably, not every organization can do what Salesforce did. Another longer-term option is to intentionally make underrepresented (and thereby in many cases, underpaid) employees aware of existing pathways to promotion and to provide the training and opportunities they need to pursue those pathways.

Pathways for promotion need to be clear and measurable before they can be equitable. Therefore, make sure your organization is providing clear performance indicators, or competencies, that need to be met for promotion, and ensure they are applied uniformly to all (no stricter requirements for one employee over another!). Then make sure everyone knows about and understands these requirements. It can be easy for managers to share the information with their favorite reports, or the best performers, or the folks who are "around" the most (an issue that is arising more and more in hybrid work situations), but they may need help and encouragement to share it with *all* of their reports.

---

8   Check out DCI Consulting's free pay equity resources at https//www.dciconsult.com/pay-equity-resources

Here's another example: Who is going to conferences and events? One of our clients who leads DEI at a large energy and manufacturing firm broke down conference presenter data by gender and ethnicity and found that white men were being sent to conferences at a higher rate than they were represented in the organization. (And given that they are already overrepresented within the organization, that meant they were *really* overrepresented when it came to attending conferences.) The company is now being more intentional about who they send to conferences, rather than sending the same people from the same homogenous group.

INCLUSALYTICS CALLOUT

Be sure to track and monitor who's participating in professional development programs and opportunities to identify inequities. Then address those inequities by intentionally targeting underrepresented groups in future recruitment efforts.

Then there's the issue of whether or not employees themselves recognize if they meet a given competency. Most organizations have their employees complete self-evaluations, which are then factored in by their managers during performance reviews. The problem is that research shows that men are more likely to be overconfident and to appraise themselves more highly than women. Then, due to the **anchoring effect** (i.e., when we see a number, we can't help but be influenced by it), managers will ultimately reward men more than women because the men rate themselves higher and, thus, influence the managers to erroneously inflate men's scores based on biased self-assessments. Women are essentially being penalized for having more accurate self-ratings.

The solution? Have managers complete their own evaluations *before* they receive the employee's self-evaluation . . . but only after training them on these gender and other performance evaluation biases. (More on that in the next chapter.) You can also adjust the review process to include peer and even direct-report evaluations of the employee. Often called a "360 review," this process helps to provide a more complete picture of an employee and to reduce potential bias when only the manager's opinion is considered.

Finally, there's the issue of an employee truly lacking a competency in which they need to excel. Sometimes this shortcoming comes down to a lack of opportunity: the opportunity to be on a bigger, more visible project, or work with a more important client, or take on more responsibilities. Often the issue with opportunities is that a manager simply picks who to give them to—and remember that pesky influence of unconscious bias? It isn't restricted to interviewing, meaning managers might give opportunities to people they are biased toward (oftentimes, white, straight, able-bodied men) over others who are equally or even more up to the task. One solution might be to implement an application process and/or include multiple decision makers when deciding which employee gets an opportunity. This can work well for big, visible projects or even promotions, but many opportunities don't warrant such a formal or resource-intensive solution. Therefore, another solution is simply raising awareness. Just as you need to make everyone aware of what it takes to get promoted, make sure all employees are aware of the opportunities available to them. We also recommend stepping in to nudge those who aren't raising their hands. They may very well be the best person for the opportunity, but stereotype threat or **imposter syndrome**—unwarranted feelings of inadequacy—might be preventing them from taking the leap.

The other thing employees need to be made aware of is the professional development opportunities your organization provides that can help them develop any competencies they lack. And these programs cannot be one size fits all. Entry to the opportunities needs to be variable; some programs may need to be manager nominated; others can be mandated; others can permit self-nomination. Additionally, depending on the content of a professional development course, you may consider tailoring versions of it to certain underrepresented groups. We'll discuss this in greater depth in the next chapter, but a simple example would be a public speaking training: one sort of delivery may be more effective if you are training employees with a sight, hearing, or learning disability compared to if you are training employees without these challenges.

INCLUSALYTICS CALLOUT

To get employees thinking about reaching for opportunities and promotions (and then to actually help them do this), use a survey question to ask them what skills they need help developing. You can also conduct a focus group with those who are not raising their hand for professional development opportunities to find out why—and then do something about it.

Other Equity Challenges (and Opportunities)

Unbiasing processes specific to development, advancement, and compensation is important because it affects *all* employees, regardless of who they are or their status within the organization. (Remember: a rising tide lifts all boats—DEI benefits everyone!) However, there are other places where, depending on what your data reveal, equity work will yield powerful results.

One such area is paid family leave. This is a hot-button issue in the United States, where national law only requires employers (and only those with fifty or more employees) to offer new mothers twelve weeks of *un*paid leave. Compare this to the global average of twenty-nine weeks of *paid* leave, and you can see why American mothers are not only feeling frustrated, but getting left behind.

A clear way to signal to current and prospective employees that your organization values working parents is by offering paid maternity leave and, if possible, paternity leave as well. You can even consider extending this policy to not just parents, but anyone who assumes primary caregiving responsibilities for another person (e.g., an elderly, sick, or disabled loved one). This is especially important considering that primary caregivers are more likely to be discriminated against compared to nonprimary or noncaregivers, regardless of gender.

INCLUSALYTICS CALLOUT

Track who is using various benefits and collect exit interview data to confirm if people are leaving due to poor benefits or if there is a lack of awareness that certain benefits (e.g., paid family leave) are, in fact, available.

Another equity opportunity involves infrastructure, like wheelchair-accessible conference rooms and gender-inclusive bathrooms. Small efforts like ensuring easy wheelchair mobility around conference tables or removing gendered labels from restroom doors, especially single-stall restrooms, can increase feelings of comfort and belongingness among your disabled and transgender employees, respectively—thus encouraging employees to stay with an organization. After all, once you invest time and resources in getting these valuable employees hired, that's your number-one goal: ensuring that they stay.

INCLUSALYTICS CALLOUT

Survey employees and ask them if their accessibility needs are being met, and if not, what is needed. You can even get those whose needs are being met to help you identify issues others may be hesitant to call out or challenges future employees may face by asking a question like, "What are the biggest accessibility obstacles with our meeting spaces?"

This chapter by no means represents all the recruitment, selection, and retention interventions you can implement. The sky's the limit! We've offered up some of the evidence-backed diversity- and equity-related interventions we've seen work with our clients, but there are many more.

Next, we're going to tackle interventions that get at the employee experience, specifically what we can do to ensure everyone is valued, respected, seen, and heard. In other words, we're going to find ways to increase inclusion and belonging.

CHAPTER 12:
Behavior Change Interventions

Making practices, policies, and procedures more equitable is one way to demonstrate to underrepresented employees that your organization values them. The other way is to make them truly feel as though they really belong.

Remember the "seed and nurture" strategy we discussed in Chapter 11? This not only applies to fixing your **talent pipeline**, but also readying the soil in which you'll eventually plant the diverse talent you've worked so hard to obtain—your organizational culture. One of our favorite partners and **DEI** authors, Gigi Gilliard, emphasizes the importance of cultivating the soil for fostering an inclusive workplace:

> *One of the most effective early strategies for cultivating workplace inclusion is to first have conversations. We "till" or prepare the soil for more complex and layered discussions on inclusion, by first addressing (1) what we need in order to have the DEI conversations (2) what is the present desire and appetite for topics on diversity and inclusion, and finally, (3) we talk about why these conversations can be so hard. Implementing this thoughtful approach allows us to "ready the soil" for the deep growth that deeper inclusion brings!*

To help employees feel valued, respected, seen, and heard, you need to ensure that your entire workforce knows their role when it comes to incorporating inclusive behaviors into their everyday actions. This is a three-step process. First you must *set expectations*. What are you expecting people to do that is new or different from what they are already doing? These expectations will differ by job function and level, so share the overarching DEI strategy with everyone first before setting out the different expectations of individual groups. (Remember the implementation plan we discussed in Chapter 10? These communications are key.)

The second step is to ensure *capability*. Does everyone have the skills and tools they need to do what you're asking them to do? This is where training comes into play, as well as other resources like **mentorship/sponsorship**/allyship programs and **employee resource groups (ERGs)**.

Finally, there's the question of *accountability*. In other words, people need to have "skin in the game." Who is responsible for these behavior changes occurring, and what happens if the changes don't occur? What happens if they do? Making these measures and their consequences (and rewards) clear is key. If you're going to tie inclusive behaviors to, say, managers' annual performance objectives (and therefore compensation), you need to provide clear measures of what qualifies as satisfactory and unsatisfactory performance.

INCLUSALYTICS CALLOUT

There are three necessary steps for fostering more inclusive behaviors among your workforce, all of which should be measured to ensure success:

- **Expectation-setting (e.g., send out a pulse survey to see if people know and understand why the org is investing in DEI and what their role is in these efforts)**
- **Capability-building (e.g., measure the frequency in which inclusive behaviors are used before and after action-based DEI training)**
- **Accountability (e.g., set minimum percentage increase in diverse vendor spending in order for the head of procurement to receive their full end-of-year bonus)**

We've already discussed setting expectations and holding individuals accountable in earlier chapters. Here we're going to discuss the capability-building tools necessary to bridge expectations and accountability.

The Current State of Diversity Training

Diversity training is "a distinct set of instructional programs aimed at facilitating positive intergroup interactions, reducing **prejudice** and **discrimination**, and enhancing the skills, knowledge, and motivation of participants to interact with diverse others." When it comes to diversity training, there is good news and bad news. Let's start with the bad news: research shows that most diversity trainings, at least as they're being conducted right now, are not very effective. A 2019 meta-analysis of nearly five hundred studies involving eighty thousand people found that **unconscious bias** training (a common type of diversity training) did not actually change **biased** behavior. The researchers found that while diversity training programs can lead to favorable reactions and positive attitudes about workplace diversity immediately following the training, any initial behavior changes as a result of those reactions quickly decayed—meaning that workplace behaviors remained mostly unchanged despite the training.

There are a number of reasons so many diversity trainings fail. One of the top reasons is that many are held as brief, single-session events. We've said it once, and we'll say it again: you cannot apply a Band-Aid to cure cancer. In this analogy, prejudice and discrimination are the cancer. They're quietly wreaking havoc beneath the surface of your organization; whether or not you're seeing symptoms, a one-day diversity training will not cure you. Diversity training needs to be part of a well-thought-out, systematic program. And just like cancer treatment requires administering a variety of specialized procedures and medicines over time (excuse the extended metaphor), diversity training needs to be delivered multiple times, on multiple occasions, in multiple contexts, with content tailored to various groups (e.g., leadership levels or historically disadvantaged versus overrepresented groups).

Another reason most diversity training programs fail is that they tend to focus on compliance. Compliance training emphasizes behaviors to avoid, rather than teaching participants inclusive behaviors they can—and should— enact on the job. Consequently, compliance-based interventions do not create necessary, sustained behavior change among participants. This is no surprise, as compliance-based DEI is the most foundational stage in our DEIx™ **Readiness Model** we discussed in Chapter 10.

As we've made clear, **inclusion** means *action*. If you only focus on what *not* to do, you fail to equip your workforce with the knowledge and skills necessary to enact behaviors that make others feel valued, respected, seen, and heard. Inclusion is simply not the absence of exclusion or discrimination. And if you don't foster the use of inclusive behaviors—through training or otherwise—they will never become the long-term habits you need to establish an inclusive culture.

The third major shortcoming of diversity training is its susceptibility to resistance or **backlash** from the overrepresented group—namely, white males. Backlash is more likely to occur when members of overrepresented groups feel excluded from diversity efforts. A major deficiency of many diversity training programs is that they often do not account for potential backlash or potential defensiveness experienced by dominant groups who view DEI as a zero-sum game.

On the flip side, the dominant group can mistakenly be assumed to be the *only* group in need of diversity training. In these cases, the training is built strictly around that singular, overrepresented identity, with little or no consideration of the experiences and needs of other identities. This often leads to tokenizing the few—or only—members of historically disadvantaged groups present in the room, asking them to not only bear the emotional labor of sharing their perspectives but also potentially making them a monolith who is (inappropriately) expected to speak for their entire demographic group, not to mention they are not gaining any personal benefit from a training that wasn't built for their perspective. By building diversity training for the overrepresented group without considering the experiences of those from underrepresented groups, you are at risk of causing more harm than good.

Turning Diversity Training into an Effective Tool

Now that we've covered all the reasons diversity training *doesn't* work, you might be wondering why the heck organizations are still spending so much time and money on it. Part of the fervor around diversity training can be **performative** ("See, we're making an effort!") or "bandwagon-ing" ("Our competitors are doing this, so we'd better do it, too!"). However, the good news is that if it's done right, diversity training *can* work when it comes to advancing DEI, and workplace inclusion especially. If you want to change a workplace culture, you need to teach people *what* behaviors they need to change and *how* to change them—not just now, but in perpetuity.

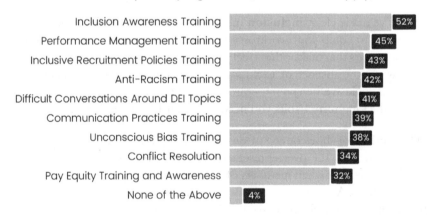

How do you incorporate DEI into your Learning and Development programs? (select all that apply)

Inclusion Awareness Training	52%
Performance Management Training	45%
Inclusive Recruitment Policies Training	43%
Anti-Racism Training	42%
Difficult Conversations Around DEI Topics	41%
Communication Practices Training	39%
Unconscious Bias Training	38%
Conflict Resolution	34%
Pay Equity Training and Awareness	32%
None of the Above	4%

Figure 17

If you remember nothing else from this chapter, remember this: awareness isn't enough. Many, many, many diversity trainings focus on awareness building (See Figure 17): "This is unconscious bias; this is why bias is bad. This is what inclusion means; inclusion is important." The problem with this approach is that just "knowing" something is not the same as "believing" it, and certainly not the same as "doing" it. And only the doing—i.e., the behaviors—will have real impact on making others feel valued, respected, seen, and heard.[9]

Knowledge, Belief, and Action

While awareness *alone* is insufficient, diversity training can and should start with awareness-building. By "awareness" we mean the basic knowledge of what DEI is, with an emphasis on our collective responsibility for building an inclusive workplace culture through our everyday actions. After all, if someone doesn't know what inclusion and **belonging** are in the first place, they're not going to be able to move forward with any sort of behavioral intervention. However, if the training is going to be effective, it needs to move from awareness to intentions and eventually to actions. According to the theory of planned behavior, *intention* to perform a behavior predicts *enacting* that behavior. In other words, to change one's behaviors, a person needs to not just be aware that they ought to do so, but to actually *intend* to do so.

To change someone's intentions—and ultimately behaviors—you need to affect their knowledge, beliefs, and attitudes. Awareness is part of this (how we define diversity, what is inclusion), but the best diversity training goes beyond imparting merely **conceptual** knowledge. For instance, research has found that diversity trainings that use a perspective-taking approach (i.e., intentionally building participants' understanding about the experiences of others) positively affect participants' attitudes and behaviors. In our work as DEI scientist-practitioners, sustained behavior change is the primary goal of effective DEI training, although it may be necessary to build up to behaviors by changing beliefs and attitudes first.

To achieve the intended knowledge-based, attitudinal, and ultimately behavioral outcomes you are hoping for, here are some evidence-based best practices for diversity training to consider including when putting together a program.

9   Design your organization's DEI training for *impact* by completing Worksheet #12 of the Inclusalytics Workbook, available at www.inclusalytics.com/workbook

Integrated Training

Diversity training can be done in one brief session (as a "check-the-box" event) or it can be integrated with other diversity-related initiatives as one of many pieces of a robust (and data-driven!) DEI strategy. You can guess which method is more effective—the latter. Here's why:

First, the integrated approach yields a greater impact than conducting a stand-alone training because it signals ongoing commitment and support for DEI by upper management and the organization at-large. Second, components of a multipronged initiative—including the diversity training itself—can work together synergistically to complement and support one another. For example, let's say that the data an organization collected shows that leaders are not acting inclusively. They therefore undergo a training on inclusive behaviors. Part of that training teaches leadership how sponsorship is an effective way to pull more diverse leaders up the ranks, and even helps them practice strategies to begin sponsoring lower-level, high-potential employees from historically disadvantaged groups. After that training, the organization announces a new sponsorship program that will be led by these inclusivity-committed leaders and will target underrepresented groups. When members of certain groups begin to receive support from sponsors, they may feel empowered to call for an employee resource group that creates a forum and safe space for their respective identity groups. What's more, these groups could also feed data back into the organization itself to foster **equity** and even business-related outcomes (more on this later). Sitting in a classroom for a few hours once a year cannot hope to achieve these sorts of compounding, sustainable results—but it can serve as a catalyst to spark more long-term, high-impact DEI initiatives.

Length of Training

And as with all training programs, DEI or otherwise, more practice equals better skill development. Specifically, Katerina Bezrukova and colleagues found that longer diversity trainings are more likely to result in participants using their learned DEI knowledge, attitudes, and skills back on the job. When it comes to DEI training, practice does make perfect (or at least better).

Still, not all diversity training sessions need to be days or even hours long. Consider how "safety moments" are commonly used to build a culture of safety in workplaces at high risk for accidents (e.g., manufacturing or construction). A safety moment, or safety chat, provides a brief safety pointer (two to five minutes long) that happens at the beginning of a meeting or shift. Its purpose is to be both educational and to remind workers of the importance of being safe at work. During the pandemic, Google's culinary staff repurposed their safety moments into a DEI learning opportunity space (which made a lot more sense for a bunch of chefs working from home who didn't face the daily risk of hurting themselves in the kitchen). Team members took turns sharing "**DEI moments**" at the beginning of meetings, during which they held brief discussions or presentations about DEI-related subjects. Other organizations that have reached a more advanced readiness stage on their DEI journey should similarly consider integrating DEI moments into their team meetings as well.

Training Delivery Method

In-person instruction—whether it's a few minutes or a few hours long—is just one delivery method for DEI training. It's a fine method, but using it alone is unlikely to yield the results you're looking for. Research shows that using multiple training techniques (e.g., live discussion, role playing, interactive technology, written material, videos) is more effective than using only one learning method. Multiple techniques can appeal to different learning preferences, which makes the training more likely to "stick" at both individual and group level. In a nutshell, different people like to consume learning content differently. The more options for how participants interact with and consume the training content, the more effective your training will be.

Spaced Learning

In addition to varying the *type* of training, spreading training content over time and providing it in more bite-sized chunks will also make the learning stickier (i.e., more likely to be retained and utilized back on the job). The distribution of learning over time is called **spaced learning**. The advantage to this approach is that the overall "training time" can stay the same (e.g., three hours total), but breaking it up into smaller sessions over time capitalizes on the way our brains form and retrieve memories. In short, the more exposures we have to a piece of information, the more pathways our brain creates to later access that information *and* the stronger those pathways become. Training research confirms that, if possible, spaced learning is the way to go: it has been shown (by hundreds of studies) to yeild better outcomes compared to trying to cram everything into one singular session.

The advantageousness of spaced learning is why **microlearning** has become a popular training approach in recent years. Microlearning is essentially short (minutes long) pieces of training content that can be consumed quickly in the midst of a learner performing their job, as opposed to the learner needing to carve out separate time to complete the training. "Because it's shorter content, folks can engage on their own terms," says Emilie Hsieh, founder & CEO of AllieBot, an **Inclusalytics** tool that not only collects data, but pushes out DEI microlearning to its users. "For employees who are newer to DEI, they may start by just reading or reacting with a "like" or an emoji. As they become more comfortable, they're more likely to comment with a follow-up question or a thoughtful response. Over time, some employees even start posting their own resources for other team members to read, and move from passive consumer to active participant in their DEI learning."

Targeted Training

So far, we've addressed the *structure* of diversity training from a variety of angles, so now it's time to look at the *content*. When building your program, you need to ask two key questions:

Who are you training, and

What do they need?

The first and most important cohort you need to train is senior leadership. We've stressed this point already, and we'll continue to do so: if senior leaders are not on board, your DEI efforts will fail. Part of getting them on board is educating them on the concepts that drive this work (Chapter 2) and making them understand its importance to the long-term success of their organization (Chapter 3). The next step is training them on the behaviors they will need to exhibit and model for the rest of the organization. A senior DEI strategy, programs, & analytics manager at an American energy corporation emphasized the importance of this:

> *You absolutely have to have 100 percent leadership buy-in. If your leaders are not driving this, it doesn't matter what you bring into the organization; it's not going to work. They have to be driving it. They have to be walking the talk. And they have to be role modeling. Because if they're not, if I'm Joe Manager, why should I do that? My leader's not doing that. My leader hasn't given me permission to do that because they're not showing me that. It's critical.*

What type of training leaders need will depend heavily on where they are in their personal DEI journey. Similar to how organizations fall somewhere on our DEIx™ Readiness Model, individuals are on their own DEI journey as well. And the organization cannot progress to the next stage of the model if its leaders are not ready. Is the CEO still stuck on what is required by law, insisting that since the company is abiding by that, everything else is "fine"? If so, your best bet for getting a foothold might be to make the case that DEI training will support the organization's business priorities. However, you'll also want to have training to increase empathy for those who are, right at this very moment, being marginalized within the organization.

INCLUSALYTICS CALLOUT

Assess where training participants are on their individual DEI journeys and direct them to specific training tracks so the content is most relevant to the specific DEI capabilities they still need to develop.

Awareness of those marginalized individuals' experiences can, in fact, be a tool for moving leaders—and consequently their organizations—further along the DEI spectrum. With one of our clients, we presented data we'd collected to show them that Black people in the organization were not having the same experience as their non-Black counterparts. When those leaders read quotes from Black participants collected from **focus groups** and open-ended survey questions, they could no longer claim, "No one's ever told me this" or, "This doesn't happen at our organization." The truth was laid bare. With that, the next step was to engage the leaders, via training, to find ways they could demonstrate to this population that they hear them, they know what's going on, and they're going to do something about it.

The fact that leaders are going through DEI training can itself be leveraged. We encourage leaders to publicize their own training to the rest of the organization. Be transparent! This isn't something shameful that should be hidden away until you emerge as a perfect, victorious champion of DEI. That end state is a myth. But it's a goal worth striving for, so enlist your workforce to help you make the effort.

INCLUSALYTICS CALLOUT

Ask for feedback. Encourage employees to tell you how the training you're undergoing is affecting things from their perspective. Is it making a difference? Can they see any changes in you and your team? Do they feel differently about the organization or about undergoing DEI training themselves?

This method of leveraging transparency around training works from the C-suite all the way down through the entire organization. Regional directors, vice presidents, department chairs, and even (especially!) middle managers can benefit from communicating when they are undergoing DEI training. Not only will the feedback help them find their own blind spots, but asking for it will help their direct reports feel valued, respected, seen, and heard.

As we mentioned, a big reason diversity training doesn't work is because it delivers the same message and education to everyone. While this is the easiest thing to do from a delivery perspective, it doesn't make sense to have one "blanket" diversity training for everyone if you want the training to be *effective* for everyone. Underrepresented groups are having a very different experience compared to the overrepresented groups, which means that their needs are different. You don't need to teach your Black employees that their voices are often undervalued, just like you don't need to teach your trans employees how to stop discriminating against themselves. While some education is necessary (everyone has biases!), these groups would be better served by trainings that incorporate trauma healing and opportunities for their voices to be heard.

A good example of targeted diversity training is a program we built in partnership with Gigi Gilliard called "Project H.E.A.L." The purpose of this program is to provide a multistaged process by which the various members of our client organization could safely and honestly talk about their varied experiences with race, power, and **privilege**. The program consists of a series of four conversations (spaced learning!), each one structured around the needs of a certain subgroup.

In one implementation of Project H.E.A.L. we focused on addressing the unique needs of an organization's employees who identified as Black. The first conversation, "Holding Space," provided a psychologically safe space for Black employees to discuss their experiences with racism and **microaggressions** at their organization. We also asked for their suggestions about what others should know or do to better serve the Black community. The second conversation, "Executive-Level Dialogue," involved sharing and discussing themes and anonymized quotes that arose from the Holding Space session with the organization's top executives. This was then parlayed into "All Leader-Level Dialogues," whereby every people manager in the organization was trained in practical techniques that we developed from the prior two conversations. Finally, in a "Listen and Support" session, we shared what was learned and actionable next steps with the workforce at-large.

As you can see, each session was tailored to the group it intended to engage. (We used Black employees in this scenario, but this could be changed to any underrepresented group.) Moreover, these individual sessions inform one another. Conducting a chronological sequence of training isn't always possible or practical, but we highly recommend collecting feedback, whether during or after training, to inform future trainings.

INCLUSALYTICS CALLOUT

Whenever a training is conducted, it is best to include a pre- and post-assessment to assess the impact of the training. For example, with Project H.E.A.L. we ask participants to respond to survey items before and after its implementation, such as:

- I know how to support my most vulnerable colleagues in times of crisis.
- I feel supported by my manager in times of crisis.

The pre-assessment can be conducted as close as possible to (but not after!) the very first session. The post-assessment should be conducted three to six months after the training concluded.

Mandatory vs. Voluntary Participation

This last diversity training element we'll discuss is a tricky one. On one hand, mandating diversity training sends a strong signal that the organization's leadership is serious about DEI. However, you do risk the possibility of backlash, or **entrenchment**, (i.e., reinforcing someone's prejudiced beliefs by attempting to change them). On the other hand, if you make the program strictly voluntary, you risk engaging only those who have already bought into the value of DEI, while missing a large swath of people who (mistakenly) think, "I'm not biased," or, "This DEI stuff doesn't apply to me." A solution, therefore, might be to make participation voluntary, but to have senior leaders present and involved in—or, for virtual deliveries, visibly championing—every training. This uses role modeling and subtle influence to help push people toward doing what you want them to do without "forcing" them.

Ultimately, it might not matter which method you choose. Bezrukova and colleagues' (2016) meta-analysis found no statistical differences in behavioral, cognitive, or attitudinal learning between groups that were required to attend diversity training and groups that attended voluntarily. However, this applies only to "diversity training at-large." Everyone in an organization needs foundational DEI training, so participation in such a program can be voluntary or mandatory. Yet only those who are fully bought into DEI and are prepared to be DEI champions should enroll in allyship training—meaning that this type of training *must* be voluntary. You cannot mandate that someone become an ally. Therefore, whether you make DEI training voluntary or mandatory also depends on the content of the training and its target audience.

Tying Training to Performance

At this point, you might have created the most effective training in the world: it's integrated and ongoing; it tailors content for employees at different levels and of different identities, and it is strategically mandatory or voluntary based on the content and target audience. However, if you don't hold people *accountable*, they're going to ignore what they've learned. After all, they have a lot to do already! And behavior change is hard, especially in the workplace.

⌐ INCLUSALYTICS CALLOUT ⌐

When developing your training, consider how you will tie it to performance and what metrics you can use to hold individuals accountable for their actions.

A national retailer client of ours is currently in the process of developing a training with an emphasis on behavior change accountability. We're helping them build a weeklong racial bias training aimed at reducing racial profiling, a common unintended consequence of loss-prevention policies intended to stop potential shoplifters. (Believe it or not, the most likely shoplifter is white!) The retail workers will watch short videos about racial profiling and then have a short conversation with their coworkers about what they learned in the videos. The final video of the week will come directly from the CEO, who will share that the company will be tracking racial profiling complaints made to their reporting hotline. Our plan for accountability is that store managers will be held accountable for the overall percentage of complaints going down, with a portion of their bonus attached.

This program hits all the key points we've covered. It targets a specific group within the organization (retail workers) and addresses a particular behavior (racial profiling). It is backed by top leadership at the company (as demonstrated by the CEO message), it is tied to measurable behavior change (measured via hotline complaints), and it uses real consequences (i.e., bonuses) to hold managers accountable. The final question: Will it work? To help determine this, we are going to establish a pre-intervention baseline—the number of racial profiling complaints that were filed the six months prior to the training. If that number goes up after another six months, our client will need to get a read on employee sentiment to see whether the training resulted in any retaliation (intentional or not). If the number stays the same, the company may need to wait a bit longer and remeasure to see whether the intervention is having an impact (especially after some managers don't receive their bonuses!), or it may need to begin examining why the training is not having its desired effect. Finally, if the numbers go down, great. But they can't take their foot off the gas; employee turnover means that there will forever be new employees in need of training. And who are these new employees? What are their identities? There is always work to be done. And training is only one tool in your DEI behavior-change toolbox. Let's now explore other evidence-based DEI interventions at your disposal.

CHAPTER 13:
DEI Interventions—More Than Just Training

Outside of training individuals in an organization to act more inclusively, there are other ways to increase feelings of **belonging** among underrepresented groups.

Employee Resource Groups (ERGs)

Another way to foster **inclusion** and belonging is through the use of **employee resource groups (ERGs)**. As we mentioned earlier, ERGs are voluntary, employee-led groups of individuals who join together based on common interests, backgrounds, or demographic factors such as gender, race, or ethnicity. There can be any number of these groups within an organization, and they can be categorically broad—e.g., multicultural, disability—or more specific—e.g., Latinas, people with neurodivergence.

Benefits of ERGs

ERGs benefit organizations in a number of ways. For one, they give marginalized individuals a space where they feel safe and included. Employees are able to use these spaces to bond and connect with other employees who share their identity, creating a sense of community and belonging. Whenever we speak with ERG members and ask them their favorite part of being in an ERG, the response is almost always something along the lines of, "I love getting to see and connect with people who look like me!"

Not only do ERGs foster a sense of belonging for underrepresented employees, they provide a platform these employees can use to make their voices heard. Previously we discussed gathering insights into employee experience through survey data. **Quantitative data** tells you "what" is going on in your organization. However, it's not always easy to get information from the people being affected by **discrimination** and marginalization, and they may not respond to your survey. Even if you do get responses, that data is limited. Rather than relying solely on incomplete survey answers, **DEI** leaders can get real-time feedback from ERGs and hold two-way conversations about interventions that are being considered or have already been implemented. If you want to know whether something you're doing is making a difference, the best way is to ask the people it's intended to affect! Relatedly, ERGs are useful for disseminating information to hard-to-reach groups. It's common for an ERG to contain a fraction of that group's overall population within the organization. However, you can bet that there are unofficial ERGs elsewhere, and members from the formal group will be able to tap into those and inform them of opportunities or initiatives you've shared. For example, this would be useful when trying to recruit **focus group** participants using the **snowball** method we discussed in Chapter 7.

Lastly, ERGs also benefit the organization just as much as—potentially even more than—they benefit the individuals who comprise them. ERGs are often tapped for feedback on how to improve DEI at the organization, particularly for employees and customers who share that ERG's identity. They can assist with anything from sourcing talent to providing feedback on a company's products or services. Or they can help with retaining people who belong in this target group across the organization. At DICK'S Sporting Goods, for instance, the "Mom Squad" ERG not only successfully campaigned for lactation rooms in the company's corporate offices, they also influenced the creation of spaces for nursing mothers throughout stores and distribution centers too. Meanwhile, the company's Black Leadership Network consults with the marketing team on ideas for DICK'S annual Black History Month campaign. In essence, ERGs give employees who don't feel heard or who feel uncomfortable speaking up in a larger setting the opportunity to share their opinions and experiences and to watch their feedback bubble up to leadership and effect real change.

If you're not yet convinced of the usefulness of ERGs, consider this: research shows that ERGs result in increased employee well-being, diversity of thought, and a fostering of equitable workplace climates. Not surprisingly, nearly every DEI leader we spoke to during the writing of this book said that their organization has ERGs. The only ones who didn't were those at organizations that were so small that forming a separate employee subgroup didn't make practical sense. (A group has to be more than one person!) Here are some best practices DEI leaders use when forming, managing, and empowering their ERGs.

Creating an ERG: Finding and Filling the Need

It makes sense to form an ERG when the need arises. The trick is identifying that need. (Obviously you can't go ask an ERG that doesn't exist if there's a need for an ERG!)

One way to uncover this need is to look at specific survey items. You don't need to specifically ask whether individuals desire an ERG (although that is certainly an option); low subgroup scores on specific items will shine light on which groups may benefit most from an ERG and the resources it provides. Here are a few examples:

- "I know what it takes to be promoted at the organization."
- "I am satisfied with the level of communication between senior leadership and employees within my area of the organization."
- "I feel heard at work."

If you find that a certain demographic of respondents is answering negatively to these sorts of questions, it might be time to form an ERG. However, don't just stop at using subgroup differences in survey data as being sufficient evidence to roll out a new ERG. This is where you take the "what" you learned in survey data to follow up with the "why" in interviews and focus groups. Just because you identified a need for an ERG doesn't necessarily mean people in a certain group *want* an ERG. Do the necessary follow-up to ensure that this would be a wanted and valuable mechanism for people who share a certain identity to gather and leverage for the benefits we previously discussed.[10]

Another popular option is to hand the reins to your employees! ERGs are employee led, after all. Many organizations have a standard structure in place for ERGs, and then it is the responsibility of the employees to reach out and ask to start the process of creating a group. This method is advantageous because the employees spearheading the group's creation are naturally lined up to lead and manage the group, so you won't need to find people who are interested in filling this role and leading the charge.

Sharing Information with ERGs

Let's say your friend wants to make you dinner, so they ask if you have any restrictions. You reply, "Yep, so be careful." Now they have no idea what to make! What they need is for you to be specific and say, "I'm allergic to shellfish."

The same holds true for ERGs: you need to share data—specific data. You can't just say, "We have a **diversity** problem," because without seeing the data underlining the specific problem, ERGs can't be effective.

Some organizations hold their DEI data close to the chest, and we understand why. But if you're asking ERGs to help you make progress on DEI initiatives,

---

10   Ready to start (or refresh) ERGs at *your* organization? Then complete Worksheet #13 of the Inclusalytics Workbook, available at www.inclusalytics.com/workbook

then they need to be privy to, at the very least, the data relevant to them. For example, let's say you have an ERG for **Latiné** employees, and in your DEI survey you see that many Latiné employees feel they cannot speak up because they fear retaliation. At a minimum, it would be pertinent to share the survey results for that item—specifically the results from the Latiné group—with the ERG. It would be even better if you shared those scores in comparison to other groups; that way the ERG could see how Latinés' responses compare to the rest of the organization. They can then provide more of the "why" behind these findings, as well as provide ideas to create more **psychological safety** for the Latiné population within the organization, which can then be spread throughout the organization through communications campaigns and/or diversity training content.

INCLUSALYTICS CALLOUT

Share relevant data with ERGs to involve them in further identifying the problems at hand and then providing recommendations for possible solutions.

Providing Resources: Purpose, Money, and Power

Along with data, ERGs need other resources. One of the most important but often neglected ways of providing those resources is a business purpose that ties them to the organization's bottom line. As we discussed earlier, ERGs can have any number of organizational benefits, from helping with talent management to marketing to learning and development. Whatever the purpose is, leadership needs to know it, understand it, and perceive it as valuable so that when business is slow and budget line items are getting cut, ERGs are *not* one of the first initiatives to go. This is why a best practice of ERGs is creating a charter that clearly states the purpose and objective of the ERG, in addition to how it will operate within that organization.

Executives need to put their money where their mouth is and provide real dollars to ERG efforts. Each ERG should have its own budget in order to be empowered to do the work that will make a difference to the organization.

An example of what an ERG can do with data plus a budget comes from Amazon, which launched a women's ERG in response to demonstrated need within one area of the company. That ERG then used **engagement** survey data to guide the creation of events (for which they had a budget) for the coming calendar year. The survey data revealed that women were running into barriers caused by a lack of communication, so the ERG held professional development sessions and networking events to address some of those communication breakdowns. It worked: in the next engagement cycle, women's engagement scores went up.

ERGs also need a budget because the leaders deserve to be paid for their time. (Otherwise, you are asking marginalized employees to do extra work for free, which perpetuates inequity!) If you can't directly pay ERG leaders, then at a bare minimum, this work needs to be made part of their official job responsibilities. This does *not* mean merely adding the role to their existing responsibilities; hours need to be *re*allocated to make space for the ERG work.

Finally, in addition to purpose and money, ERGs need power. They need to not just be seen as valuable, but *treated* as valuable. They need to be able to spend their budgets as they see fit and empowered to take action without too many layers of red tape. One network employee manager we interviewed shared that her company's individual ERGs all report to a global ERG leadership team, which is led by a designated president. The company's DEI team provides the ERGs with a budget, and the global ERG president—*not* anyone on the DEI team—manages how that budget is spent. This is an example of the autonomy ERGs ought to have.

INCLUSALYTICS CALLOUT

Be sure that your ERGs are measuring their success as they go. Sample metrics include number of ERG members and attendance at events. If they make business recommendations, the organization should measure the impact of those suggestions and share it back with the ERG. For example, if your women's ERG established a sponsorship program to help increase the number of women in leadership, you could provide a yearly update on how many new women have entered leadership roles and how many were participants in that sponsorship program. You should also communicate ERG-driven DEI "wins" to other internal and external stakeholders as well, such as in your annual report (Chapter 9).

Mentorship, Sponsorship, and Allyship

The final category of intervention we'll cover that's been proven to advance DEI outcomes among underrepresented groups is what we call the three "-ships" of individualized support: **mentorship**, **sponsorship**, and allyship. While all three are valuable, we're only going to endorse two—sponsorship and allyship. Read on to see why.

Overmentored, Undersponsored

Mentorship is a relationship in which a more knowledgeable or experienced person (mentor) guides and nurtures the professional development of another, less experienced person (mentee) outside the normal manager-subordinate relationship. Sponsorship, on the other hand, is a relationship that produces objective career benefits for the person being sponsored, commonly called a protégé. In a nutshell, a sponsor uses their power and status to advocate for a protégé's career advancement. This might include nominating the protégé for management roles, inviting them to high-status networking events, and sharing examples of their performance and capabilities with influential peers. In essence, these actions help the protégé access resources and experiences that might otherwise be out of reach, and they help to increase the protégé's reputation and value without their having to promote themselves.

The difference between these two roles should be clear: a mentor helps an individual improve themselves; a sponsor helps that person succeed by performing external, public actions that help elevate the individual's career. Mentorship is saying "I can help you develop XYZ skills," whereas sponsorship is saying, "I believe in this person and am staking my reputation on supporting them."

The fact that sponsorship yields tangible benefits for the protégé is why we endorse it over mentorship—whether it's called "sponsorship" or not. In a survey of MBA graduates, Catalyst (a nonprofit dedicated to greater workplace inclusion) found that women had mentors who were more likely to coach and advise, while men's mentors actively advocated for their protégés. In effect, the men had sponsors, while the women had mentors. And unsurprisingly, after just two years, the men—who, again, had *sponsors*—were found to have received 15 percent more promotions than the women—who had mentors. It's no surprise that experts recommend DEI programs "upgrade mentorship to sponsorship" as a key action organizations should take to promote diversity and inclusion.

The Magic of Allyship

If sponsorship is about leveraging one's status and network to advance another person's career, allyship takes that a level up by having allies explicitly supporting those from historically disadvantaged groups from which the ally doesn't belong. Whereas sponsors and proteges can share the same identity (e.g., an LGBTQ+ executive sponsoring a lower-level LGBTQ+ employee), allies and partners cannot. *Allyship* is a relationship between an ally and their partner whereby the two work together toward the shared goal of fairness, **equity**, and social justice.

In a sponsorship, a sponsor needs to hold a position of power (often sitting in a high-up leadership role) to effectively advocate for the protégé. However, anyone can be an ally. The key requirement of allyship is that the partner (the individual being served) not share the same identity as the ally. Allyship works via the ally leveraging their in-group status and **privilege** to help the partner overcome inequities they face. Therefore, you don't need organizational power to be an ally, you need privilege—something everyone has, since privilege is multifaceted (e.g., access to people, resources, and other benefits one's in-group status can provide).

To be an ally means:

1. Using your privilege and status…

2. To support and advocate for…

3. Someone who doesn't share a key part of your identity, for example:
   - Male allies for women
   - White allies for People of Color
   - Straight allies for LGBTQ+ individuals

The magic of allyship lies in something called the *contact hypothesis*, which essentially says that contact between interpersonal groups can reduce **prejudice** between those groups. Otherwise known as "exposure," intentionally and regularly interacting with people who belong to groups that we hold **unconscious biases** against is the only consistently proven strategy for actually reducing one's unconscious bias toward that group. This evidence-based finding is the holy grail of bias mitigation, a key outcome of most DEI efforts, yet a sorely underutilized approach. This is why we focus so much on allyship—these authentic partnerships between individuals of different identity groups—when it comes to our behavior-change solutions for more mature DEI programs.

Setting Up Sponsor and Ally Programs

The best way to foster sponsors and allies is to create a culture where people naturally build these relationships. However, it is possible to create a formal program as well. If you go that route, start by involving the right people. This will include the DEI team and HR, also perhaps ERGs, talent management, and other relevant groups and departments. For a sponsorship or allyship program to work, it needs buy-in and designated leaders to build the program and assess impact. So you need DEI champions who can encourage sponsors/allies to participate, people who will encourage protégés/partners to participate, people who can help guide the experience, and, of course, people who will gather data to see how well the program is working.

Next, you'll need to determine a structure that's standardized and scalable. There are a number of considerations here, starting with how you'll match individuals together. Once paired, we strongly recommend coaching the sponsor/ally on basing the relationship and resulting actions taken on the unique and specific needs of the protégé/partner. This can be as simple as providing a conversation guide, goal-setting tool kit, or a more robust training program to set up these partnerships for success. Then you'll want to determine how protégés/partners will obtain visibility and job experience from the program. This can be formalized and embedded as part of a standardized process you provide, or it can be left up to each pair with specific outcomes that are measured as the program progresses. As your program becomes more robust, you might also consider tying it to protégés'/partners' development plans so they get formally rewarded—ideally with a future promotion—for their efforts.

Finally, communicate the program to leaders within your organization as well as to employees. This harkens back to the groups you involved at the outset—ERGs, for instance, can likely reach groups who might not otherwise respond to a more generalized communication about sponsorship/allyship opportunities. No matter what sort of initial engagement you get, you can always continue to build. So continue to measure—and communicate—what's working and what's not because you never know who might be one step away from joining the program.

INCLUSALYTICS CALLOUT

Track and monitor who is taking advantage of formal (or informal) sponsorship and allyship opportunities to ensure that the most underrepresented groups in the organization are set up to benefit the most.

Expand Beyond Your Organization

One last thing to note is that mentorship, sponsorship, and allyship programs don't always have to be internal to support an organization's goals. In 2020, Salesforce announced that it was committing $100 million to Black-owned businesses and $100 million to underrepresented minority-founded companies by 2023. As part of this racial justice and equity initiative, the company launched a Black-owned business mentor/sponsor program in July 2021. Each participant in its twenty-five-business cohort was paired with a senior Salesforce mentor who provided ongoing coaching, as well as a Salesforce executive sponsor. While this program may not *directly* affect Salesforce's internal supplier diversity goals, it will help to build a strong pipeline of Black-owned businesses and suppliers, which will improve a company's diverse supplier options in the long run.

INCLUSALYTICS CALLOUT

Measure the diversity of your vendors (e.g., those who hold women- or minority-owned certifications) year over year to track whether those numbers are increasing and by how much.

Is It Working?

Over the last three chapters we have covered a number of DEI interventions, from recruitment to selection to retention strategies and from diversity trainings to ERGs to "the three -ships." Now that you've put interventions in place to increase the diversity of your workforce and retain those individuals through equity and inclusion efforts, you need to ask (and will inevitably be asked by higher-ups): "Is what we're doing *working?*" Your intent might be good, but you need to know whether you're having impact. This takes us back to measurement.

Measurement is not easy, nor is analysis. "Is it working?" is a simple question with a complex answer, as you've possibly noticed from the analysis chapters and various **Inclusalytics** callouts throughout the book. This is also why we recommend bringing in external partners with DEI and data analysis expertise: because most organizations find that when they try to tackle DEI alone, they wind up with one of two answers: "We don't know," or, "No."

Building a data-based DEI program can feel overwhelming. You might feel lost, frustrated, or all of the above. But instead of backing out, ask for help— because DEI is work worth doing, and doing *right*. The more improvements you make, the more welcoming your organization will be to all your employees, especially currently underrepresented individuals. And as research has shown, the more diversity you have, the better your organization will perform.

CHAPTER 14:

The Future of Inclusalytics

If the last thirteen chapters feel like a lot to take in, don't worry! You've just spent a few hours reading about concepts and processes we were trained to perform in graduate school and further developed and refined throughout our entire careers. Hopefully, though, you now feel better prepared to do the following:

- Collect **diversity**, **equity**, and **inclusion** data
- Derive meaningful insights from those data
- Communicate your findings to all relevant stakeholders
- Implement effective data-driven **DEI** interventions
- Measure the impact of your interventions (i.e., begin the cycle again!)

Yet what we've written isn't the end-all be-all of **Inclusalytics**. The fact is, there is no "end." This is just the beginning. In a few short years, we'll likely need to update much of this book, because DEI as a field is moving at an incredibly rapid pace. Most organizations already possess a surplus of data; the future is in the science and art of using the right technology to better capture and organize that data and turn it into actionable insights.

Note that we didn't just write, "The future is in the technology," but that the future is in the art and science of *using* that technology. Technology is only as good as what you do with it. For instance, if you don't have the know-how to select between various DEI or HR tech vendors—of which there are increasingly many—and how to monitor the technology you choose, **bias** can creep in and start wreaking havoc on your DEI program. After all, technology is built by humans—and humans have biases!

"When you're building AI, especially for human applications, you must have data scientists that nearly mirror the demographics of the people you're serving," says Michael Ogunsanya, CEO and cofounder of AI-driven Inclusalytics company MindStand. "Otherwise, you create homogenous tools that only service the people building them."

Michael experienced this himself when he was invited to visit one of the largest players in Silicon Valley. Everyone on this vast and beautiful campus seemed enthusiastic, energetic, and eager to work there—evidence of a company successfully building a positive, inclusive culture. It wasn't until Michael attempted to wash his hands in one of the bathrooms that he discovered all was not quite as idyllic as it seemed. When he waved his hand under the sink's sensor, it didn't recognize his dark skin tone. He had to cover his hand in a white tissue for the sensor to work. "It felt ironic and alarming to be at such a tech giant and to still experience technological bias at this high level," said Ogunsanya.

So, bias still exists, and technology is just as susceptible to it. Therefore, we believe the future of Inclusalytics is not merely tied to rapidly improving technology, but to organizations doing the following: creating more accountability and transparency; experimenting with different interventions; connecting with one another; measuring **intersectionality**; and developing sustainable systems, processes, and workflows that directly contribute to DEI goals and outcomes. Because, after all, doing DEI right means embedding it into every aspect of how your organization functions.

Measurable Accountability and Transparency

One more time for the people in the back: accountability is key to making DEI stick. Importantly, it needs to be data-driven accountability. It needs to be measurable. And it needs to start with top leadership.

Leaders are the guardians of culture, and culture is the cornerstone of DEI outcomes. If leaders don't embody certain values and enact corresponding behaviors, no one will (why should they?), and the status quo will prevail. *That's* why it's so important to start with leadership accountability. They need to be held accountable with data, and they need to have skin in the game to actually follow through with DEI efforts.

DOW, a leader in corporate DEI efforts, sets a good example of DEI leadership accountability. In the 2021 CEO for Action for Diversity & Inclusion Summit, DOW's chief diversity officer, Karen Carter, shared how they use a scorecard to evaluate progress on the company's stated DEI metrics. They've tied C-suite bonuses to this scorecard. If the company isn't meeting its DEI goals, the leaders feel the effect right where it matters—in their wallet.

DOW also uses transparency, another principle we keep hammering home, to ensure accountability. The company reports their findings publicly every quarter and publishes a comprehensive DEI report annually. Are the leaders succeeding? Is the organization achieving its stated DEI goals? If they're not, everyone—

meaning not only current and prospective employees, but also competitors, startups, keyboard warriors, and even friends and family—can see. Public reckoning can be a powerful motivator. Use it.

Experimentation Means Failure—Embrace it

This is going to sound easy for us to say, given that we are trained psychologists, but it's the truth: as a DEI leader, you need to think of yourself as a scientist. Scientists recognize that failure is an inevitable step in the process of learning. It's expected and even embraced, because failure provides valuable information, and these important lessons help move you toward success. DEI work is no different. Successful Inclusalytics requires experimentation; therefore, you need to accept that your experiments won't always succeed.

Get comfortable with failing. Come to expect it. Getting things wrong, figuring out why, making changes, and going through the process again and again is what you're here for. (And, if you need guidance during any stage of that process, that's what *we're* here for.)

We've had clients fail to see the results they wanted. We've had clients see an intervention that worked great for one group fail miserably for another. Organizations that make measurable progress toward DEI goals are the ones that use those failures to inform what they do next. Sometimes the intervention itself doesn't work, but more often than not, the issue lies in not collecting the right—or any!—data to accurately measure what is and is not working so the organization can pivot accordingly. Some of our clients had to go back and gather data differently. Others had to gather data from different groups. Still others had to be patient and gather more data over a longer period of time. The more open and agile you can remain, and the more willing you are to try new things, the quicker you can get through the failures to find the interventions that result in the DEI outcomes you're striving to achieve.

Making Connections, Sharing Resources

In addition to learning from failure, the other thing successful organizations are doing is connecting with others. The fact is, no single organization has fully figured out how to get DEI right. Often, this comes down to lack of resources. Money is typically the first resource that comes to mind, but it isn't the only one—not by a long shot. DEI leaders need access to people, spaces, insider knowledge, specialized skill sets, and case studies that can serve as a guiding light for what works (and what doesn't). That's why we need to connect with each other and share our own learnings and discoveries. (Honestly, it's why we wrote this book!) A win for one is a win for all. Because even if your organization was as diverse, inclusive, and equitable as it could possibly be—which we all know it isn't (no one's is)—there are your vendors to consider, and your customers, and the communities where you operate. The work is never done, and no one person or organization can do it alone. Partnership and collaboration are key.[11]

One group that ties together collaboration and leadership accountability is CEO Action for Diversity & Inclusion. This coalition comprises "the largest collection of business leaders from various industries openly committing to sharing successful diversity and inclusion initiatives as well as lessons learned to share with the collective business community". CEOs pledge to perform certain actions within their own organization, and they commit to sharing their findings and strategies with other members. Pledges are great, but the true work lies in keeping those connections alive and collaborating with, working with, and learning from each other. When the follow-up doesn't happen, that's when pledges become **performative** rather than resulting in real change.

There are also campaigns and movements that bring together industry-based organizations to share resources and DEI best practices that work within their unique context. One such campaign is Open to All, a customer service-specific "national nondiscrimination campaign based around the idea that everyone should be welcome regardless of race, ethnicity, national origin, sex, sexual orientation, gender identity and expression, immigration status, religion, or disability." There's also *The ACT Report,* published by the Catalyze Tech Working Group, which presents data, research, and best practices from dozens of top businesses and nonprofits in the tech industry. These are the sorts of initiatives that you can both participate in and draw from. You can provide value—and even nonprivileged data—as you benefit from using others'—even competitors'!—insights to improve your own DEI strategy. It's collaboration that helps everyone level up.

The Importance of Identities and Intersectionality

If you're already elbow deep in data, you will have begun to recognize that the future of DEI lies in intersectionality, because there are so, so many identities to explore with different groups having different needs.

In the United States, most organizations focus their DEI efforts primarily on gender, race, and sexual identity (LGBTQ+), what we like to call the "big three." A quick glance at American history reflects these foci: we've had the women's rights

---

11 Unsure of who you should have in your broader DEI network? Work through the social network map in Worksheet #14 of the Inclusalytics Workbook, available at www.inclusalytics. com/workbook

movement, the Stonewall Uprising, and now the Black Lives Matter movement. While each movement has resulted in some progress, none has led to complete equality; the conversation continues today, the work forever incomplete. Yet we cannot stay limited to just these three identities. We must also look at how they intersect with each other and with the many other identities that intersect with the "big three": age, veteran status, neurodiversity, mental illness, caregiver status . . . the list goes on and on. And in the workplace, there are even more identities to consider when you add in tenure, department, location, etc.

Right now, very few organizations are capturing these expansive, intersectional categories. When we partner with an organization, we make sure to measure many different identities to ensure that we're prioritizing the most disadvantaged groups based not on who DEI leaders and executives think needs the most support, but on feedback from the employees themselves. Leaders might assume that women need DEI support, for instance, but when breaking the data down by race, we might find that Asian men are demonstrating the least **engagement** and have the greatest frustrations within the organization. If we broke the data down even further, adding in age and tenure, we might be able to get even more targeted with our intervention. This is why intersectionality matters!

To serve the many populations working within an organization, we must start by giving people the opportunity to share their many identities. This is done by collecting the data necessary to explore real group differences among intersectional identities. Yet *opportunity* to share one's identities is not enough. The organization also needs to create a culture where people *feel comfortable* supplying that personal information. Part of creating that culture is being transparent about why you are collecting the data and following through with actions based on your findings. Only by creating this safe environment will we be able to collect the accurate, complete data that we need to make meaningful changes for the groups that could benefit most.

Building a Sustainable DEI Future

Workers need to feel comfortable sharing their information, and they also need to feel that they are sharing it for a purpose. They deserve a satisfactory answer to the question, "What's in it for me?" In other words, data collection needs to be mutually beneficial.

Amber Thompson, founder of the equity-building workplace reporting platform de-bias, points out that a lot of DEI data collection focuses overwhelmingly on *taking* data from marginalized groups—and this is a serious shortcoming:

Data collection needs to be participatory. This isn't just us taking; this is about us giving. The process of me collecting data allows the person giving the information to learn, to be engaged, and to participate in visioning their future.

Ultimately, it's only by actively involving your workforce in DEI initiatives that you will be able to sustain them. Everyone needs to be on board—leadership, workers, and not least of all, the owner of your organization's HR analytics.

For Inclusalytics to come to life, you need to have a very close partnership with the people who own your organization's HR data. Assuming they have the right analytical skill set, they can pull the data, help clean it, and help generate usable outputs. (And if they don't have the right skill sets, that's where consultants like us come in.) But they're looking to *you* for the right research questions. So take this book, figure out where you are on your DEI journey, and start formulating your questions. What has been done so far? What do you still need to know? And who can you partner with to get data-based answers to solve the most pressing DEI issues?

Not a Moment, but a Movement

We will finish with one final assertion: DEI is not a fad. The Great Resignation of 2020 and 2021 showed us that. For better or for worse, COVID-19 changed the game. As the world shut down and then gradually reopened, workers realized the power they have to choose where and how they work. By quitting in droves, they have demonstrated their determination to work for organizations that make them feel valued, respected, seen, and heard. They're refusing to work for less. Therefore, if you want to keep people at your organization, you need to listen to them and enact changes that will make them want to stay. DEI is no longer just nice to have; it's critical for the success of any organization in the twenty-first century.

If it sounds like we're asking for a utopia, we're not. It's unrealistic to believe in a future where equality exists for everyone, everywhere, all the time, even within a single organization. But that doesn't make efforts to get as close to that idealistic future as possible any less worthwhile. DEI work is aspirational work. We are making progress that affects people's lives and well-being. And as with any other transformational change, you need everyone to prioritize it, to conduct ongoing research, and to assess and iterate as you go. That requires data. That requires Inclusalytics.

GLOSSARY

Adverse Impact A substantially different rate of selection in hiring, promotion, or other employment decision which works to the disadvantage of members of a race, sex, or ethnic group. Also referred to as disparate impact

Analytics The application of statistics to detect patterns in data that can then be interpreted to drive meaningful and actionable predictions and insights

Anchoring Effect When an initial value influences a subsequent value

Anonymous Information that is unnamed or unidentified

Backlash Social and economic penalties for defying stereotypical expectations

Belonging The feeling that one's authentic self is valued, respected, seen, and heard

Bias An inclination or predisposition for or against something (see also "Unconscious bias")

BIPOC Acronym for Black, Indigenous, People of Color

Commitment An employee's personal feeling of responsibility toward their organization and the people with whom they work

Conceptual Knowledge The knowledge of, or understanding of, concepts, principles, theories, etc. Also referred to as declarative knowledge

Confidential Information that is kept secret or private

Construct Confusion A lack of clarity or shared understanding around terminology, especially terminology specific to a given discipline such as I-O psychology

DEI Diversity, equity, and inclusion

DEI/Diversity Moment A brief two-to-five-minute discussion or presentation about DEI-related subjects, held at the beginning of a meeting or work shift

DEI Dashboard Visual summary of the DEI, HR, and other data you have collected (or are collecting) and analyzed

Dependent Variable The variable being measured or tested in an experiment; it is the variable that depends on other factors

Design Thinking An iterative problem-solving approach that favors action over discussion

Discrimination Perceived unfair or biased treatment based on membership in a particular social group

Diversity The presence (and amount) of difference among a group within a given setting

Effect Size The size of a difference between populations or the strength of an association between two variables in the same population

Employee Resource Group (ERG) Identity- or experience-based group that builds community, provides support to its members, and contributes to the personal and professional development of its members in the workplace

Engagement The mental and emotional connection employees feel toward their workplace, the work they do, and the people with whom they do it

Entrenchment Reinforcing someone's prejudiced beliefs by attempting to change them

Equity The fair treatment of all employees regarding the accessibility of information, opportunities, and resources

Equity Audit An examination of all policies, practices, and procedures, both formal and informal, to determine if they present a barrier to the hiring, advancement, or full inclusion of employees who belong to disadvantaged groups

Focus Group Organized discussions with a selected group of individuals (typically who share some trait) to gain information about their views and experiences of a topic

Groupthink When the desire for group harmony overrides rational decision-making

Impact Measures Well-defined metrics that assess the effect a program or intervention has on the population it targets

Imposter Syndrome When an individual doubts their knowledge, skills, and abilities despite evident success

Inclusion (or Inclusive Behaviors) Actions that make others feel valued, respected, seen, and heard

Industrial-Organizational (I-O) Psychologists Psychologists who apply evidence-based practices to improve the well-being and performance of people and the organizations that employ them

Inclusalytics The process of applying statistics to DEI data to detect patterns, make predictions, select evidence-based interventions, and assess the impact of those interventions to advance workplace inclusion

Intersectionality The interconnected nature of social categorizations such as race, class, and gender, regarded as creating overlapping and interdependent systems of discrimination or disadvantage

Latiné A gender-neutral form of the word Latino

Mentorship A relationship in which a more knowledgeable or experienced person guides and fosters the professional development of a less knowledgeable/experienced person outside the normal manager-subordinate reporting structure

Microaffirmations Small acts, which are often hard to see, that are public and private, often unconscious but very effective, which occur whenever people wish to help others to succeed

Microaggressions Brief and commonplace daily verbal, behavioral, or environmental indignities, whether intentional or unintentional, that communicate hostile, derogatory, or negative slights and insults toward others

Microlearning Short pieces of training content that can be consumed quickly

Nonresponse Pattern The failure of a survey participant to respond to the survey as a whole or select items that the respondent is eligible to answer

Nudges Reminders that affect a person's behavior in a seemingly predictable way without changing incentives or removing options from their potential choices

Operationalize Clearly defining a term and how it will be experienced and used

Panel Interview An interview that includes multiple interviewers, usually three to five

Performative DEI When an organization or person conveys a commitment to diversity, equity, and inclusion but takes no practical actions to contribute to the achievement thereof

Positive Presuppositions Framing a statement or question to presume positive intent

Prejudice An unjustified or incorrect attitude (usually negative) toward an individual based solely on the individual's membership of a social group

Privilege The advantages one has over others based on their associations with the overrepresented group (e.g., white, straight, male, cisgender, able-bodied). Privilege can also be earned, like wealth or having an advanced degree

Psychological Safety The ability to speak honestly or make mistakes without fear of negative consequences or repercussions

Psychometrics A scientific discipline concerned with the construction of assessment tools, measurement instruments, and formalized models that may serve to connect observable phenomena (e.g., responses to items in an IQ test) to theoretical attributes (e.g., intelligence)

Pulse Surveys Short microsurveys deployed at regular intervals or following a particular action that an individual has performed

Quantitative Data Data that can be expressed numerically

Qualitative Data Descriptive data comprised of words or language

Representation Ensuring that your workforce demographics represent the people in your market, your industry, and the population in geographic areas your organization operates

Readiness Model A model indicating how prepared an organization is to pursue a particular intervention. Sometimes also referred to as a "maturity model"

Reliability A quality of a research measure whereby it consistently has the same results if it is used in the same situation on repeated occasions

Snowball Sampling A recruitment technique in which research participants are asked to assist with recruiting other potential participants for the test or study

Spaced Learning When learning is spread out over multiple intervals. Also called "distributed learning"

Sponsorship A relationship that produces objective career benefits for the person (protégé) being sponsored

Static Report A time-bound snapshot of data at one moment in time and the insights gleaned from it

Statistical Significance When a result from data generated by testing or experimentation is unlikely to be explained solely by chance or random factors

Stereotype Threat A feeling of fear or anxiety of confirming a negative stereotype about the marginalized group to which one belongs

Structured Interview An interview process that involves issuing the same questions in the same order to every interviewee and using the same rubric to score every interview

Survey Fatigue When your audience becomes bored, uninterested, or annoyed by your surveys

Talent Pipeline The pool of individuals who are qualified and prepared to fill relevant job positions when they fall vacant

Targeted Universalism The necessity of having both an overarching goal that involves everyone—building more diverse, equitable, and inclusive organizations—while also taking targeted approaches to meeting the unique needs of specific populations within that broader community

Thematic Analysis Looking at one or several open-ended questions on a survey, or reading through transcripts from interviews or focus groups, and looking for common themes

Tokenism The practice of doing something (such as hiring a person who belongs to a marginalized group) only to prevent criticism and give the appearance that people are being treated fairly

Triangulation A process of data verification that uses multiple methods and data sources to study the same thing

Unconscious Bias Also called "implicit bias"; subconscious beliefs that are likely to show up as unfair decisions, behaviors, and outcomes. In the context of DEI, unconscious bias commonly results in discrimination against individuals from underrepresented groups (see also "Bias")

Validity The extent to which a concept is accurately measured in a study

Verification The process of checking, confirming, making sure, and being certain

Virtue Signaling Also called "moral grandstanding"; a contribution that individuals make to convince others with an underlying motivation of recognition

REFERENCES

CHAPTER ONE

[1] Hunt, V., Prince, S., Dixon-Fyle, S., & Yea, L. (2015, January). Delivering through diversity. McKinsey & Company.

[2] Carr, E. W., Reece, A., Rosen Kellerman, G., & Robichaux, A. (2019, December). The value of belonging at work. *Harvard Business Review*.

CHAPTER TWO

[1] Oxford University Press. (2021, June). Intersectionality, n. In *OED Online*.

[2] Steinmetz, K. (2020, February 20). She coined the term "Intersectionality" over 30 years ago. Here's what it means to her today. *Time Magazine*.

[3] Roberson, Q., Ryan, A. M., & Ragins, B. R. (2017). The evolution and future of diversity at work. *Journal of Applied Psychology, 102*(3), 483–499.

[4] Horne, R. M., Johnson, M. D., Galambos, N. L., & Krahn, H. J. (2018). Time, money, or gender? Predictors of the division of household labour across life stages. *Sex Roles, 78*(11), 731–743.

[5] Del Boca, D., Oggero, N., Profeta, P., & Rossi, M. (2020). Women's and men's work, housework and childcare, before and during COVID-19. *Review of Economics of the Household, 18*(4), 100–017.

[6] Hegewisch, A., & Tesfaselassie, A. (2019). *The gender wage gap 2018: Earnings differences by gender, race, and ethnicity. Fact sheet, IWPR #C484*. Institute for Women's Policy Research.

[7] Chen, C. & Tang, N. (2018). Does perceived inclusion matter in the workplace? *Journal of Managerial Psychology, 33*(1), 43–57.

[8] Mor Barak, M. E., Lizano, E. L., Kim, A., Duan, L., Rhee, M.-K., Hsiao, H.-Y., & Brimhall, K. C. (2016). The promise of diversity management for climate of inclusion: A state-of-the-art review and meta-analysis. *Human Service Organizations: Management, Leadership & Governance, 40*(4), 305–333.

[9] Merriam-Webster. (n.d.). Tokenism. In *Merriam-Webster Learner's Dictionary*.

[10] Kanter, R. M. (1977). *Men and women of the corporation*. Basic Books.

[11] Casad, B. J., & Bryant, W. J. (2016). Addressing stereotype threat is critical to diversity and inclusion in organizational psychology. *Frontiers in Psychology*.

[12] Emmerich, A. I., & Rigotti, T. (2017). Reciprocal relations between work-related authenticity and intrinsic motivation, work ability and depressivity: A two-wave study. *Frontiers in Psychology, 8*, Article 307.

[13] Kernis, M. H., & Goldman, B. M. (2006). A multicomponent conceptualization of authenticity: Theory and research. In M. P. Zanna (Ed.), *Advances in experimental social psychology*, Vol. 38 (pp. 283–357). Elsevier Academic Press.

[14] Lirio, P., Lee, M. D., Williams, M. L., Haugen, L. K., & Kossek, E. E. (2008). The inclusion challenge with reduced-load professionals: The role of the manager. *Human Resource Management, 47*, 44–61.

[15] Rowe, M. (2008). Micro-affirmations and micro-inequities. *Journal of the International Ombudsman Association, 1*(1), 45–48.

[16] Pierce, C. M. (1974). Psychiatric problems of the Black minority. In S. Arieti (Ed.), *American Handbook of Psychiatry* (pp. 512–523). Basic Books.

[17] Sue, D.W., Capodilupo, C. M., Torino, G. C., Bucceri, J. M., Holder, A. M. B., Nadal, K. L., & Esquilin, M. (2007). Racial microaggressions in everyday life: Implications for clinical practice. *American Psychologist, 62*(4), 271–286.

[18] Shore, L. M., Randel, A. E., Chung, B. G., Dean, M. A., Holcombe, Ehrhart, K., & Singh, G. (2011). Inclusion and diversity in work groups: A review and model for future research. *Journal of Management, 37*, 1262–1289.

[19] Brown, J. (2017). *Inclusion: Diversity, the new workplace & the will to change*. Publish Your Purpose Press.

CHAPTER THREE

[1] Cletus, H., Mahmood, N., Umar, A., & Ibrahim, A. (2018). Prospects and challenges of workplace diversity in modern day organizations: A critical review. *HOLISTICA– Journal of Business and Public Administration, 9*(2) 35–52.

[2] Herring, C. (2009). Does diversity pay?: Race, gender, and the business case for diversity. *American Sociological Review, 74*(2), 208–224.

[3] Hofhuis, J., van der Rijt, P. G., & Vlug, M. (2016). Diversity climate enhances work outcomes through trust and openness in workgroup communication. *SpringerPlus, 5*(1), 714.

[4] Inegbedion, H., Sunday, E., Asaleye, A., Lawal, A., & Adebanji, A. (2020). Managing diversity for organizational efficiency. *SAGE Open.*

[5] Li, W., Wang, X., Haque, M. J., Shafique, M. N., & Nawaz, M. Z. (2020). Impact of workforce diversity management on employees' outcomes: Testing the mediating role of a person's job match. *SAGE Open.*

[6] Rich, B. L., Lepine, J. A., & Crawford, E. R. (2010). Job engagement: Antecedents and effects on job performance. *Academy of Management Journal, 53*(3), 617–635.

[7] Schaufeli, W. B., Salanova, M., González-Romá, V., & Bakker, A. B. (2002). The measurement of engagement and burnout: A two-sample confirmatory factor analytic approach. *Journal of Happiness Studies: An Interdisciplinary Forum on Subjective Well-Being, 3*(1), 71–92.

[8] Harter, J., & Mann, A. (2017, April 12). The right culture: Not just about employee satisfaction. *Gallup.*

[9] Knight, C., Patterson, M., & Dawson, J. (2017). Building work engagement: A systematic review and meta-analysis investigating the effectiveness of work engagement interventions. *Journal of Organizational Behavior, 38*(6), 792–812.

[10] Edelbroek, R., Peters, P., & Blomme, R. J. (2019). Engaging in open innovation: The mediating role of work engagement in the relationship between transformational and transactional leadership and the quality of the open innovation process as perceived by employees. *Journal of General Management, 45*(1), 5–17.

[11] Rahmadani, V. G., Schaufeli, W. B., Stouten, J., Zhang, Z., & Zulkarnain, Z. (2020). Engaging leadership and its implication for work engagement and job outcomes at the individual and team level: A multi-level longitudinal study. *International Journal of Environmental Research and Public Health, 17*(3), 776.

[12] Hunt, V., Prince, S., Dixon-Fyle, S., & Dolan, K. (2020). Diversity wins. *McKinsey.*

[13] Leonard, J. S., & Levine, D. I. (2006). The Effect of Diversity on Turnover: A Large Case Study. ILR Review, *59*(4), 547–572.

[14] Ferrazzi, K. (2015, March 25). Technology can save onboarding from itself. *Harvard Business Review.*

[15] Hackenberg, J. (2021, April 29.) Brands, you need to listen to the conscious consumer of the future. *Forbes.*

[16] McFeely, S., & Wigert, B. (2019, March 13). This fixable problem costs U.S. businesses $1 trillion per year. *Gallup.*

[17] Sandler, R. (2020, October 8). 60 employees leave Coinbase over CEO's Pledge to be apolitical. *Forbes.*

[18] Miller, J. (2021, February 18). For younger job seekers, diversity and inclusion in the workplace aren't a preference. They're a requirement. *Washington Post.*

[19] Levine, S. R. (2020, January 15). Diversity confirmed to boost innovation and financial results. *Forbes.*

[20] Hofhuis, J., van der Rijt, P. G., & Vlug, M. (2016). Diversity climate enhances work outcomes through trust and openness in workgroup communication. *SpringerPlus, 5*(1), 714.

[21] Li, W., Wang, X., Haque, M. J., Shafique, M. N., & Nawaz, M. Z. (2020). Impact of workforce diversity management on employees' outcomes: Testing the mediating role of a person's job match. *SAGE Open.*

[22] Patrick, H. A., & Kumar, V. R. (2012). Managing workplace diversity: Issues and challenges. *SAGE Open.*

[23] White, K., McCoy, M., Love, K., Eun, J. K., Bruce, E., & Grable, J. (2019). The role of signaling when promoting diversity and inclusion at the firm level: A financial advisory professional case study. *Advances in Business Research, 9*(1), 1–16.

[24] Kim, S. S., & Gelfand, M. J. (2003). The influence of ethnic identity on perceptions of organizational recruitment. *Journal of Vocational Behavior, 63*(3), 396–416.

[25] Perkins, L. A., Thomas, K. M., & Taylor, G. A. (2000). Advertising and recruitment: Marketing to minorities. *Psychology & Marketing, 17*(3), 235–255.

[26] Harter, J. K., Schmidt, F. L., Agrawal, S., Plowman, S. K., Blue, A., Plowman, S., Josh, P. & Asplund, K. (2020). The relationship between engagement at work and organizational outcomes. Gallup Poll Consulting University Press.

[27] Sorenson, S., & Garman, K. (2013, June 11). How to tackle U.S. employees' stagnating engagement. *Gallup.*

[28] Funk, K., & Parker, C. (2017, December 14). Gender discrimination comes in many forms for today's working women. *Pew Research Center.*

[29] Funk, C., & Parker, K. (2018, January 9). Blacks in STEM jobs are especially concerned about diversity and discrimination in the workplace. *Pew Research Center.*

[30] Human Rights Campaign Foundation. (n.d.). *Discrimination against transgender workers.*

[31] Dhanani, L. Y., Beus, J. M., & Joseph, D. L. (2017). Workplace discrimination: A meta-analytic extension, critique, and future research agenda. *Personnel Psychology, 71,* 147–179.

[32] Caprino, K. (2018, October 26). New data reveals the hard costs of bias and how to disrupt it. *Forbes.*

[33] Baldoni, J. (2013, July 4). Employee engagement does more than boost productivity. *Harvard Business Review.*

[34] Harter, J., & Mann, A. (2017, April 12). The right culture: Not just about employee satisfaction. *Gallup.*

[35] Schneider, B., Ehrhart, M. G., & Macey, W. H. (2011). Perspectives on organizational climate and culture. In S. Zedeck (Ed.), *APA handbook of industrial and organizational psychology, Vol. 1. Building and developing the organization* (pp. 373–414). American Psychological Association.

[36] Greenwald, A. G., & Krieger, L. H. (2006). Implicit bias: Scientific foundations. *California Law Review, 94*(4), 945–967.

[37] Glazer, E., & Francis, T. (2021, June 2). CEO pay increasingly tied to diversity goals. *The Wall Street Journal.*

CHAPTER FOUR

[1] Hinchliffe, E. (2021, June 2). The female CEOs on this year's Fortune 500 just broke three all-time records. *Fortune.*

[2] U.S. Equal Employment Opportunity Commission. (n.d.) *EEOC Data Collection.*

CHAPTER FIVE

[1] Chin, M. H., & Chien, A. T. (2006). Reducing racial and ethnic disparities in health care: an integral part of quality improvement scholarship. *BMJ Quality & Safety,* 15, 79–80.

[2] The Race Equ(al)ity Project. (n.d.) Race equality index.

[3] Dickey, M. R. (2021, May 11). Racial equity at tech companies is hard to measure. This index wants to change that. *Protocol.*

[4] Bloomberg. (n.d.). *Gender-equality index: Invested in a more equal future.*

[5] Disability:IN. (n.d.) Disability equality index.

[6] Human Rights Campaign. (n.d.). Corporate equality index 2021.

CHAPTER SIX

[1] Judd, S., O'Rourke, E., & Grant, A. (2018, March 14). Employee surveys are still one of the best ways to measure engagement. *Harvard Business Review.*

[2] Raykov, T., & Marcoulides, G. A. (2011). *Introduction to psychometric theory.* Routledge.

[3] Heale, R., & Twycross, A. (2015). Validity and reliability in quantitative studies. *Evidence-Based Nursing, 18*, 66–67.

[4] Morse, J. M., Barrett, M., Mayan, M., Olson, K., & Spiers, J. (2002). Verification strategies for establishing reliability and validity in qualitative research. *International Journal of Qualitative Methods 1*(2), 13–22.

[5] Strauss, A., & Corbin, J. (1998). *Basics of qualitative research: Techniques and procedures for developing grounded theory.* Sage Publications, Inc.

[6] Hinkin, T. R. (1995). A review of scale development in the study of behavior in organizations. *Journal of Management, 21*, 967–988.

CHAPTER SEVEN

[1] Gibbs, A. (1997). Focus groups. *Social Research Update, 19.*

[2] Kitzinger J. (1995). Qualitative research: Introducing focus groups. *BMJ, 311,* 299.

[3] Cordivano, S. (2019, October 31). Understanding employee resource groups: A guide for organizations. *Medium.*

CHAPTER EIGHT

[1] Shoobridge, G. (2017, May 30). *Ensure "authentic and meaningful" employee survey participation.* LinkedIn.

[2] U.S. Equal Employment Opportunity Commission. (1979). *Questions and answers to clarify and provide a common interpretation of the uniform guidelines on employee selection procedures.*

[3] Saldaña, J. (2016). *The coding manual for qualitative researchers.* SAGE Publishing.

[4] Tracy, S. J. (2013). *Qualitative research methods: Collecting evidence, crafting analysis, communicating impact.* Wiley-Blackwell.

[5] Schmidt, F. L., & Hunter, J. E. (1974). Racial and ethnic bias in psychological tests: Divergent implications of two definitions of test bias. *American Psychologist, 29*(1), 1–8.

[6] Oxford University Press. (2021, June). Intersectionality, n. In *OED Online.*

[7] Northon, L., Dooney, J., Esen, E., Kong, W., and Mariotti, A. (2016, November). *2016 human capital benchmarking report.* Society for Human Resource Management.

[8] Brannon, T. N., Carter, E. R., Murdock-Perriera, L. A., & Higginbotham, G. D. (2018). From backlash to inclusion for all: Instituting diversity efforts to maximize benefits across group lines. Social Issues and *Policy Review, 12*(1), 57–90.

CHAPTER NINE

[1] Ries, E. (2011). *The Lean Startup.* Crown Business.

[2] Tamir, C. (2021, March 25). *The growing diversity of black America.* Pew Research Center.

[3] Bowles, J., Dvorkin, E., & Shaviro, C. (2020, August). *Stark disparities in employment and wages for Black New Yorkers.* Center for an Urban Future.

[4] Payne, D. (2011, July 12). How many contacts does it take before someone buys your product? *Business Insider.*

CHAPTER TEN

[1] Pedulla, D. (2020, May 12). Diversity and inclusion efforts that really work. *Harvard Business Review.*

[2] Ashikali, T., Groeneveld, S., & Kuipers, B. (2021). The Role of Inclusive Leadership in Supporting an Inclusive Climate in Diverse Public Sector Teams. Review of Public Personnel Administration, 41(3), 497–519.

[3] Kozlowski, S. W., & Doherty, M. L. (1989). Integration of climate and leadership: Examination of a neglected issue. *Journal of Applied Psychology, 74*(4), 546–553.

[4] Gjerde, S., & Alvesson, M. (2020). Sandwiched: Exploring role and identity of middle managers in the genuine middle. Human Relations, 73(1), 124–151.

[5] Pedulla, D. (2020, May 12). Diversity and inclusion efforts that really work. *Harvard Business Review.*

[6] AnitaB.org. (2020). Top companies for women technologists: Building a more inclusive future.

[7] Victorian Equal Opportunity and Human Rights Commission. (2013.). (rep.). *Waiter, is that inclusion in my soup? A new recipe to improve business performance* (pp. 1–32). Deloitte Australia.

[8] Bourke, J., and Titus, A. (2020, March 6.) The key to inclusive leadership. *Harvard Business Review.*

[9] Tosi, J., & Warmke, B. (2016). Moral grandstanding. *Philosophy & Public Affairs, 44*(3), 197–217.

CHAPTER ELEVEN

[1] Leonard, P., Halford, S., & Bruce, K. (2016). 'The New Degree?' Constructing Internships in the Third Sector. *Sociology, 50*(2), 383–399.

[2] Stewart III, S., Pinder, D., & Chui, M. (2021, July 14). Closing the job mobility gap between Black and white Americans. *Harvard Business Review.*

[3] O'Donnell, B. (2021, April 26). Looking to level up? Amazon, Google, Microsoft and more offer training programs. *USA Today.*

[4] White House Office of Science and Technology Policy. (2016, November). *Diversity, equity, and inclusion in science and technology: Action grid.*

[5] Zhao, J. (2019, March). *These companies are tying executive bonuses to diversity goals.* Payscale.

[6] Staats C, Patton C. State of the science: implicit bias review: the Ohio State University Kirwan Institute for the study of race and ethnicity. OH: The Kirwan Institute for the Study of Race and Ethnicity at The Ohio State University, 2013; 1–102.

[7] Baltimore Tracks. (n.d.). *Our commitments.*

[8] American Council on Education. (2017). *Educational attainment, by race and ethnicity.*

[9] Mohr, T. S. (2014, August 25). Why women don't apply for jobs unless they're 100% qualified. *Harvard Business Review.*

[10] Gaucher, D., Friesen, J., Kay, A.C. (2011). Evidence that gendered wording in job advertisements exists and sustains gender inequality. *Journal of Personality and Social Psychology, 101*(1), 109–128.

[11] Morse, G. (2016, July-August). Designing a bias-free organization. *Harvard Business Review.*

[12] Rockwood, K. (2018, January 22). *Hiring in the age of ageism.* Society for Human Resource Management.

[13] Carnes, M., Devine, P. G., Isaac, C., Manwell, L. B., Ford, C. E., Byars-Winston, A., Fine, E., & Sheridan, J. (2012). Promoting institutional change through bias literacy. *Journal of Diversity in Higher Education, 5*(2), 63–77.

[14] Solomon, B., Hall, M., & Muir, C. (2021). When and why bias suppression is difficult to sustain: The asymmetric effect of intermittent accountability. *Academy of Management Journal.*

[15] Kulik, C. T, Perry, E. L., & Bourhis, A. C. (2000). Ironic evaluation processes: effects of thought suppression on evaluations of older job applicants. *Journal of Organizational Behaviour, 21*, 689–71.

[16] Goldin, C., & Rouse, C. (2000, September). Orchestrating impartiality: The impact of "blind" auditions on female musicians. *American Economic Review, 90*(4), 715–741.

[17] Wharton School. (2016, March 24). *"Gender equality by design": Building a more inclusive (and productive) workplace.*

[18] Casad, B. J., & Bryant, W. J. (2016). Addressing stereotype threat is critical to diversity and inclusion in organizational psychology. *Frontiers in Psychology.*

[19] Nguyen, H. H. D., & Ryan, A. M. (2008). Does stereotype threat affect test performance of minorities and women? A meta-analysis of experimental evidence. *Journal of Applied Psychology, 93*(6), 1314–1334.

[20] Schmader, T., & Hall, W. (2014). Stereotype threat in school and at work: Putting science into practice. *Policy Insights from the Behavioral and Brain Sciences, 1*(1), 30–37.

[21] Inzlicht, M., & Ben-Zeev, T. (2000). A threatening intellectual environment: Why females are susceptible to experiencing problem-solving deficits in the presence of males. *Psychological Science, 11*, 365–371.

[22] Spencer, S. J., Steele, C. M., & Quinn, D. M. (1999). Stereotype threat and women's math performance. *Journal of Experimental Social Psychology, 35*(1), 4–28.

[23] Ellis, J., Otugo, O., Landry, A., & Landry, A. (2020). Interviewed while Black. *The New England Journal of Medicine, 383*, 2401–2404.

[24] King, E., & Gilrane, V. (2015). *Social science strategies for managing diversity: Industrial and organizational opportunities to enhance inclusion.* Society for Human Resource Management and Society for Industrial and Organizational Psychology.

[25] Steele, D. M., & Cohn-Vargas, B. (2013). *Identity safe classrooms: Places to belong and learn.* Corwin.

[26] Vohra, N., Chari (Coordinators), V., Mathur, P., Sudarshan, P., Verma, N., Mathur, N., Thakur, P., Chopra, T., Srivastava, Y., Gupta, S., Dasmahapatra, V., Fonia, S., & Gandhi, H. K. (2015). Inclusive Workplaces: Lessons from Theory and Practice. *Vikalpa, 40*(3), 324–362.

[27] Morse, G. (2016, July-August). Designing a bias-free organization. *Harvard Business Review.*

[28] Wiesner, W. H., & Cronshaw, S. F. (1988). A meta-analytic investigation of the impact of interview format and degree of structure on the validity of the employment interview. *Journal of Occupational Psychology, 61*, 275–290.

[29] Inzlicht, M., & Ben-Zeev, T. (2000). A threatening intellectual environment: Why females are susceptible to experiencing problem-solving deficits in the presence of males. *Psychological Science, 11*, 365–371.

[30] Google. (n.d.). Guide: Use structured interviewing.

[31] Ellis, J., Otugo, O., Landry, A., & Landry, A. (2020). Interviewed while Black. New England Journal of Medicine, 383(25), 2401–2404.

[32] Fine, E., & Handelsman, J. (2012). Searching for excellence and diversity: A guide for search committees. Women in Science & Engineering Leadership Institute.

[33] O'Meara, K. A., Culpepper, D., & Templeton, L. L. (2020). Nudging toward diversity: Applying behavioral design to faculty hiring. *Review of Educational Research, 90*(3), 311–348.

[34] Toosi, N. R., Mor, S., Semnani-Azad, Z., Phillips, K. W., & Amanatullah, E. T. (2019). Who Can Lean In? The Intersecting Role of Race and Gender in Negotiations. Psychology of Women Quarterly, 43(1), 7–21.

[35] Leibbrandt, A., & List, J. A. (2015). Do women avoid salary negotiations? Evidence from a large-scale natural field experiment. *Management Science 61*(9), 2016–2024.

[36] O'Brien, K. R., Scheffer, M., van Nes, E. H., & van der Lee, R. (2015). How to Break the Cycle of Low Workforce Diversity: A Model for Change. PloS one, 10(7), e0133208.

[37] Stewart, S., Pinder, D., & Chui, M. (2021, July 14). *Closing the job mobility gap between black and White Americans.*

[38] Payscale. (2021.) *The state of the gender pay gap in 2021.*

[39] Liden, R. C., & Graen, G. (1980). Generalizability of the vertical dyad linkage model of leadership. *Academy of Management Journal, 23*(3), 451–465.

[40] Ring, P., Neyse, L., David-Barett, T., & Schmidt, U. (2016). Gender Differences in Performance Predictions: Evidence from the Cognitive Reflection Test. *Frontiers in Psychology, 7,* 1680.

[41] Bohnet, I., (2016). *What Works: Gender Equality by Design.* Harvard University Press.

[42] Morse, G. (2016, July-August). Designing a bias-free organization. *Harvard Business Review.*

[43] Crawford W.S., Shanine K.K., Whitman M.V., & Kacmar K.M. Examining the impostor phenomenon and work-family conflict. *J Manag Psychol.* 2016;31(2):375–90.

[44] White House Office of Science and Technology Policy. (2016, November). *Diversity, equity, and inclusion in science and technology: Action grid.*

[45] Miller, C. C. (2021, October 25). The world "has found a way to do this": The U.S. lags on paid leave. *The New York Times.*

[46] Kingsbury, M. A. (2019). Expanding Understanding of Motherhood Penalty: How Gaps in Family Policies Contribute to Gaps in Old-Age Earnings in Russia. *Frontiers in Sociology, 4,* 67.

[47] Henle, C. A., Fisher, G. G., McCarthy, J., Prince, M. A., Mattingly, V. P., & Clancy, R. L. (2020). Eldercare and childcare: How does caregiving responsibility affect job discrimination? *Journal of Business and Psychology, 35*(1), 59–83.

CHAPTER TWELVE

[1] Bezrukova, K., Spell, C., Perry, J., & Jenn, K. (2016). A meta-analytical integration of over 40 years of research on diversity training evaluation. *Psychological Bulletin, 11,* 1227–1274.

[2] Forscher, P. S., Lai, C. K., Axt, J. R., Ebersole, C. R., Herman, M., Devine, P. G., & Nosek, B. A. (2019). A meta-analysis of procedures to change implicit measures. *Journal of Personality and Social Psychology, 117*(3), 522–559.

[3] Benschop, Y., & Verloo, M. (2006). Sisyphus' sisters: can gender mainstreaming escape the genderedness of organizations? *Journal of Gender Studies, 15,* 19–33.

[4] Leslie, L. M., Mayer, D. M., & Kravitz, D. A. (2014). The stigma of affirmative action: A stereotyping-based theory and meta-analytic test of the consequences for performance. *Academy of Management Journal, 57,* 964–989.

[5] Burke, R. J., & Black, S. (1997). Save the males: Backlash in organizations. *Journal of Business Ethics, 16,* 933–942.

[6] Kaiser, C. R., Major, B., Jurcevic, I., Dover, T. L., Brady, L. M., & Shapiro, J. R. (2013). Presumed fair: Ironic effects of organizational diversity structures. *Journal of Personality and Social Psychology, 104,* 504–519.

[7] Benschop, Y., & Verloo, M. (2006). Sisyphus' sisters: can gender mainstreaming escape the genderedness of organizations? *Journal of Gender Studies, 15,* 19–33.

[8] HR. Research Institute. (2021, February). The Future of Diversity, Equity and Inclusion 2021. HR.com.

[9] Ajzen, I. (1985). From intentions to actions: A theory of planned behavior. In J. Kuhl, & J. Beckmann (Eds.), *Action control: From cognition to behavior* (pp. 11–39). Springer Verlag.

[10] Kraiger, K., Ford, J. K, & Salas, E. (1993). Application of cognitive, skill-based, and affective theories of learning outcomes to new methods of training evaluation. *Journal of Applied Psychology, 78*, 311–28.

[11] Lindsey, A., King, E., Hebl, M., & Levine, N. (2014). The impact of method, motivation, and empathy on diversity training effectiveness. *Journal of Business and Psychology, 30*, 605–617.

[12] Bezrukova, K., Spell, C., Perry, J., & Jenn, K. (2016). A meta-analytical integration of over 40 years of research on diversity training evaluation. *Psychological Bulletin, 11*, 1227–1274.

[13] Curtis, E. F., Dreachslin, J. L., & Sinioris, M. (2007.) Diversity and cultural competence training in health care organizations: Hallmarks of success. *Health Care Management Review, 26*, 255–262.

[14] Anders, E. (2004). Deliberate practice and the acquisition and maintenance of expert performance in medicine and related domains. *Academic Medicine, 71*(10), S70-S81.

[15] Kolb, A. Y., & Kolb, D. A. (2005.) Learning styles and learning spaces: Enhancing experiential learning in higher education. *Academy of Management Learning and Education, 4*, 193–212.

[16] Bjork, R. A., & Kroll, J. F. (2015). Desirable difficulties in vocabulary learning. *American Journal of Psychology, 128*, 241–252.

[17] Cepeda, N. J., Pashler, H., Vul, E., Wixted, J. T., & Rohrer, D. (2006). Distributed practice in verbal recall tasks: A review and quantitative synthesis. *Psychological Bulletin, 132*(3), 354–380.

[18] Ashikali, T., Groeneveld, S., & Kuipers, B. (2021). The Role of Inclusive Leadership in Supporting an Inclusive Climate in Diverse Public Sector Teams. Review of Public Personnel Administration, *41*(3), 497–519.

[19] Pulakos, E. D., Hanson, R. M., Arad, S., & Moye, N. (2015). Performance management can be fixed: An on-the-job experiential learning approach for complex behavior change. *Industrial and Organizational Psychology: Perspectives on Science and Practice, 8*(1), 51–76.

[20] Dabney, D. A., Hollinger, R. C., & Dugan, L. (2006). Who actually steals? A study of covertly observed shoplifters. *Justice Quarterly, 21*(4), 693–728.

CHAPTER THIRTEEN

[1] Goode, S., & Dixon, I. (2016, August 25). *Are employee resource groups good for business?* Society for Human Resources Management.

[2] Welbourne, T. M., Rolf, S., & Schlachter, S. (2017). The case for employee resource groups: A review and social identity theory-based research agenda. *Personnel Review, 46*(1), 1816–1834.

[3] (2019), "ERGs (employee resource groups) benefit employee wellbeing," Human Resource Management International Digest, Vol. 27 No. 1, pp. 45–46.

[4] White House Office of Science and Technology Policy. (2016, November). *Diversity, equity, and inclusion in science and technology: Action grid.*

[5] Montgomery, B. L., Dodson, J. E., Johnson, S. M. (2014). Guiding the way: Mentoring graduate students and junior faculty for sustainable academic careers. SAGE Open, 4(4). doi:10.1177/2158244014558043.

[6] Kirkpatrick-Husk, K. (2015). *Obtaining sponsorship in organizations by developing trust through outside of work socialization.* Digital Commons at Seattle Pacific University.

[7] Sharma, G., Narula, N., Ansari-Ramandi, M. M. & Mouyis, K. (2019). *J. Am. Coll Cardiol Case Rep. 1*(2), 232–234.

[8] Wharton School. (2016, March 24). *"Gender equality by design": Building a more inclusive (and productive) workplace.*

[9] White House Office of Science and Technology Policy. (2016, November). *Diversity, equity, and inclusion in science and technology: Action grid.*

[10] Pettigrew, T. F. (2021). Advancing intergroup contact theory: Comments on the issue's articles. *Journal of Social Issues, 77*, 258– 273.

[11] Gonzalez, A. M., Steele, J. R., & Baron, A. S. (2017). Reducing children's implicit racial bias through exposure to positive out-group exemplars. *Child Development, 88*(1), 123–130.

[12] Joy-Gaba, J. A., & Nosek, B. A. (2010). The surprisingly limited malleability of implicit racial evaluations. Social Psychology, *41*(3), 137–146.

[13] Salesforce.com. (n.d.). *Racial equity and justice.*

[14] Catalyze Tech Working Group. (2021, October). *The ACT report: Action to catalyze tech, A paradigm shift for DEI.* The Aspen Institute and Snap Inc. ACTReport.com.

[15] Dixon-Fyle, S., Dolan, K., Hunt, V., and Prince, S. (2020, May 19). *Diversity wins: How inclusion matters.* McKinsey & Company.

CHAPTER FOURTEEN

[1] CEO Action for Diversity & Inclusion. (n.d.). *FAQs.*

[2] *Open to All.* (2021).

[3] Catalyze Tech Working Group. (2021, October). *The ACT report: Action to catalyze tech: A paradigm shift for DEI.* Aspen Digital.

ABOUT THE AUTHORS

Victoria Mattingly, PhD, is founder and CEO of Mattingly Solutions, a workplace inclusion consulting firm. Holding her doctorate in organizational psychology, Dr. V was trained to turn abstract concepts like inclusion into quantifiable metrics, enabling organizations to track and assess progress toward reaching their diversity, equity, and inclusion goals. Her life's mission is to use organizational science to improve the human experience at work, especially for underrepresented groups. Based in Pittsburgh, PA, Dr. V leads a fully remote team and serves clients virtually across the US.

Sertrice Grice, MS, is cofounder and Chief Consulting Officer of Mattingly Solutions.[12] Sertrice is passionate about helping organizations use their metrics to develop data-backed diversity, equity, and inclusion strategies. She created a free broad DEI survey, an Anti-Racist Organization survey, and has helped clients create customized DEI surveys. Sertrice also writes and presents frequently on DEI matters. She is currently located in Raleigh, NC.

Allison Goldstein is a writer and editor who works with business leaders, award-winning academics, and professionals to bring their literary ideas to the world. A graduate of the University of Rochester, where she studied English and cognitive sciences, Allison has over fifteen years of experience in writing, editing, and marketing. She is based in Jersey City, NJ.

---

12 Want to explore how a partnership with Mattingly Solutions could advance DEI efforts at your organization?

- Checkout Worksheet #15 of the Inclusalytics Workbook, available at www.inclusalytics. com/workbook
- Or schedule time with us at www.mattinglysolutions.com/

Made in United States
Cleveland, OH
13 December 2024

11697455R00115